COLLECTOR'S ED

People

General Hospital

CELEBRATING 60 YEARS OF LOVE & DRAMA

SONNY FORECAST Maurice Benard's beloved mobster Sonny has found happiness with current flame Nina (Cynthia Watros).

USTRALIA
AFRICA
HAWAII
ENGLAND
HOLLYWOOD
PACIFIC OCE
MEXICO
NASHVILLE
BEECHERS CORNERS
PURITY WATER CO.
TOWNHALL
LAURELTON
GENERA HOSPITA
HARDY'S
PINE VALLEY
ELQ INDUSTRIES
AMBULANCE
LLANVIEW
WANDA'S
ORINTH
WLPC TV
FLOATING RIB RESTAURANT
EXPO
PORT CHARLES HERALD
RK
ROBERT HOLLY
ANNA DUKE
The Spa
PORT CHARLES HOTEL
LIPS
STEVE AUDREY
MONICA ALAN
BOBBIE JAKE
LUKE LAURA
RICK LESLEY
LOVERS LANE
BROWNSTONE
SD
WATERSIDE CLINIC
KELLY'S DINER
LAW OFFICE
HARBOR VIEW TOWERS
THE HAUNTED STAR

Contents

HOME SWEET HOME
For legions of the show's fans, Port Charles (seen in a quirky map from 1995) is the center of the universe.

FOR 60 YEARS, *GENERAL HOSPITAL* HAS KEPT DEVOTED FANS TUNING IN THANKS TO A CAPTIVATING MIX OF ROMANCE, DRAMA AND ESCAPISM

General *Excellence*

By **CAROLYN HINSEY**

"HOW MANY SHOWS make 60 years?" marvels Genie Francis, whose *General Hospital* character Laura represents everything that has kept millions of fans tuning into the ABC soap opera for more than 15,000 episodes—and counting! Love, loss, a summer on the run from the Mob, the biggest daytime TV marriage in history, kidnappings, a murder trial, catatonia, going over a waterfall, a secret son with a member of the Cassadine clan, a machine that could freeze the world and a hunt that is *still* going on for the Ice Princess diamond is just a fraction of the drama Laura has triumphed over since 1977, when the innocent teen set Port Charles—and eventually 30 million TV watchers at her wedding to Luke—on fire. Through it all, Francis and thousands of other talented actors have brought the Hardys, Brewers, Webbers, Spencers, Quartermaines, Scorpios, Joneses, Corinthoses and more to life, beginning with 30 minutes a day in 1963, expanding to 45 minutes in 1976 and the full hour in 1978. Credit that final expansion to Gloria Monty, who joined *GH* as executive producer when the show teetered on the brink of cancellation in 1978 and was given 13 weeks to turn it around. Monty increased the show's pace, updated sets and shot on location, introduced edgier story lines and invigorated the cast and crew by inviting their contributions (including letting them ad lib) and created daytime's first "supercouple" with married teenager Laura and troubled mobster Luke (Anthony Geary), who became so popular that Academy Award-winning movie star Elizabeth Taylor had her people call *GH*'s people to request a formal invitation to their 1981 wedding.

BRIGHT FUTURE
The show launched in black-and-white and went to color in 1967. Above: the first color title card.

Monty left for other projects in 1987, but when she returned in the 1990s her star had faded. So ABC brought in executive producer Wendy Riche and head writer Claire Labine, who ushered in a decade of dramatic social issue story lines. BJ's heart transplant, Stone dying of AIDS, Robin contracting HIV, AJ's alcoholism and Monica's breast cancer are just a few of the moving tales that kept *GH* near the top of the ratings and won a slew of Daytime Emmy Awards during that decade.

Leaner years followed, with some of the show's biggest stars let go to save money. Rebecca Herbst, who joined *GH* as Jeff Webber's 15-year-old daughter Elizabeth Webber in 1997, says that after she was fired in 2011, it was fan outcry that helped bring her back. That, and the fact that the honchos who scripted her exit were fired themselves. "It was funny," Herbst tells *People*, "There was a knock on my door: 'We made a mistake, can you come back?' I have so much appreciation for the fans' love for Elizabeth and this show."

She also appreciates current executive producer Frank Valentini, who joined *GH* in 2012 and has made it his mission to keep as many veteran actors onscreen as possible despite massive budget cuts. "Frank is super dedicated to running this ship," says Herbst, a sentiment echoed by many of her fellow actors. Tune in today and you'll not only see Elizabeth and her former mother-in-law Laura but also Robert, Anna, Felicia, Scotty, Bobbie, Lucy and Ned from the 1970s-'80s still making waves at their favorite Port Charles haunts like Kelly's Diner, the Quartermaine mansion and, of course, the GH nurses' station.

Respecting the rich history of this show is job one for the cast, crew and execs as they cruise up on six decades of "Love in the Afternoon." When the big day rolls around on April 1, 2023, Genie Francis has only one wish: "*GH* is so special and has had so many stars... [I] hope it gets the love it deserves."

Yes—and here's hoping they solve the mystery of that cursed diamond!

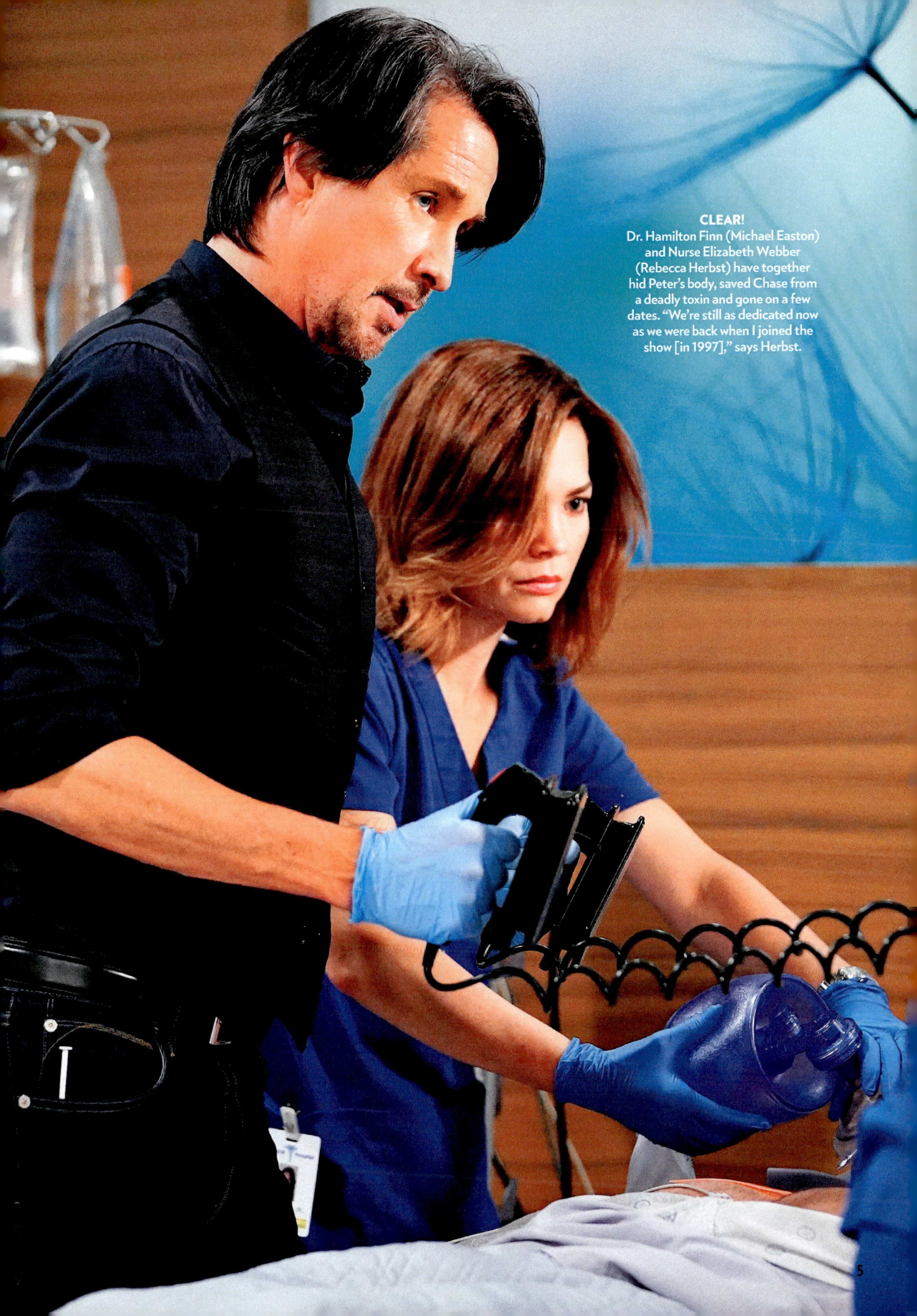

CLEAR!
Dr. Hamilton Finn (Michael Easton) and Nurse Elizabeth Webber (Rebecca Herbst) have together hid Peter's body, saved Chase from a deadly toxin and gone on a few dates. "We're still as dedicated now as we were back when I joined the show [in 1997]," says Herbst.

WHO COULD FORGET THESE SHOCKING BETRAYALS, DEVASTATING HEARTBREAKS AND ONE VERY SPECIAL WEDDING?

TOP 10

Memorable *Moments*

1

LUKE AND LAURA'S WEDDING (1981)

It's hard to explain the phenomenon of the mobbed-up disco manager Luke Spencer (Anthony Geary) and the married teenager Laura Webber (Genie Francis) going on the run in 1980, but by the time they walked down the aisle, 30 million people were tuning in, and Academy Award winner Elizabeth Taylor was crashing their nuptials. The TV milestone was filmed at the Greystone Mansion in Beverly Hills (aka the Quartermaine mansion) on a sweltering day with every major *GH* actor in attendance. There were complications (including bees swarming the wedding cake), but there was no chance of the actors' forgetting their lines, thanks to the show's demanding executive producer. "In that situation where Gloria [Monty] was on location," Francis recalls to *People*, "you were not going to be the one to screw up!"

2

STONE BATTLES AIDS (1995)

It was the most impactful story *GH* ever told: Orphan Stone Cates (Michael Sutton) experimented with drugs before falling in love with Robin Scorpio (Kimberly McCullough), and they both later tested positive for HIV—with Stone eventually contracting AIDS. Robin and Sonny cared for Stone as he battled the disease, losing his eyesight near the end. His last words were, "I see you.... Oh Robin, I see you!" "The love that poured through us that day was a reflection of the best of us, when we can see through the prejudice and fear of a disease and treat the person with compassion," McCullough wrote on Instagram in 2020. "Telling stories can be a vehicle for enlightenment, and yes, even soap operas can change the world."

3

BJ'S HEART TRANSPLANT (1994)

They set it up perfectly. Dr. Tony Jones (Brad Maule) and nurse Bobbie Spencer (Jacklyn Zeman, left, with Norma Connolly) learned their daughter BJ (Brighton Hertford) was in a bus crash and would not survive. They had only moments to make the decision to donate her heart to Tony's niece Maxie (Robyn Richards), daughter of his brother Frisco (Jack Wagner) and sister-in-law Felicia (Kristina Wagner), whose heart was failing. "Not Barbara Jean!" cried Felicia as she fell to the floor at the hospital upon learning whose heart had saved her daughter. Then Tony snuck into Maxie's hospital room to listen to his late daughter's heart beating in her chest. Can you say tearjerker?

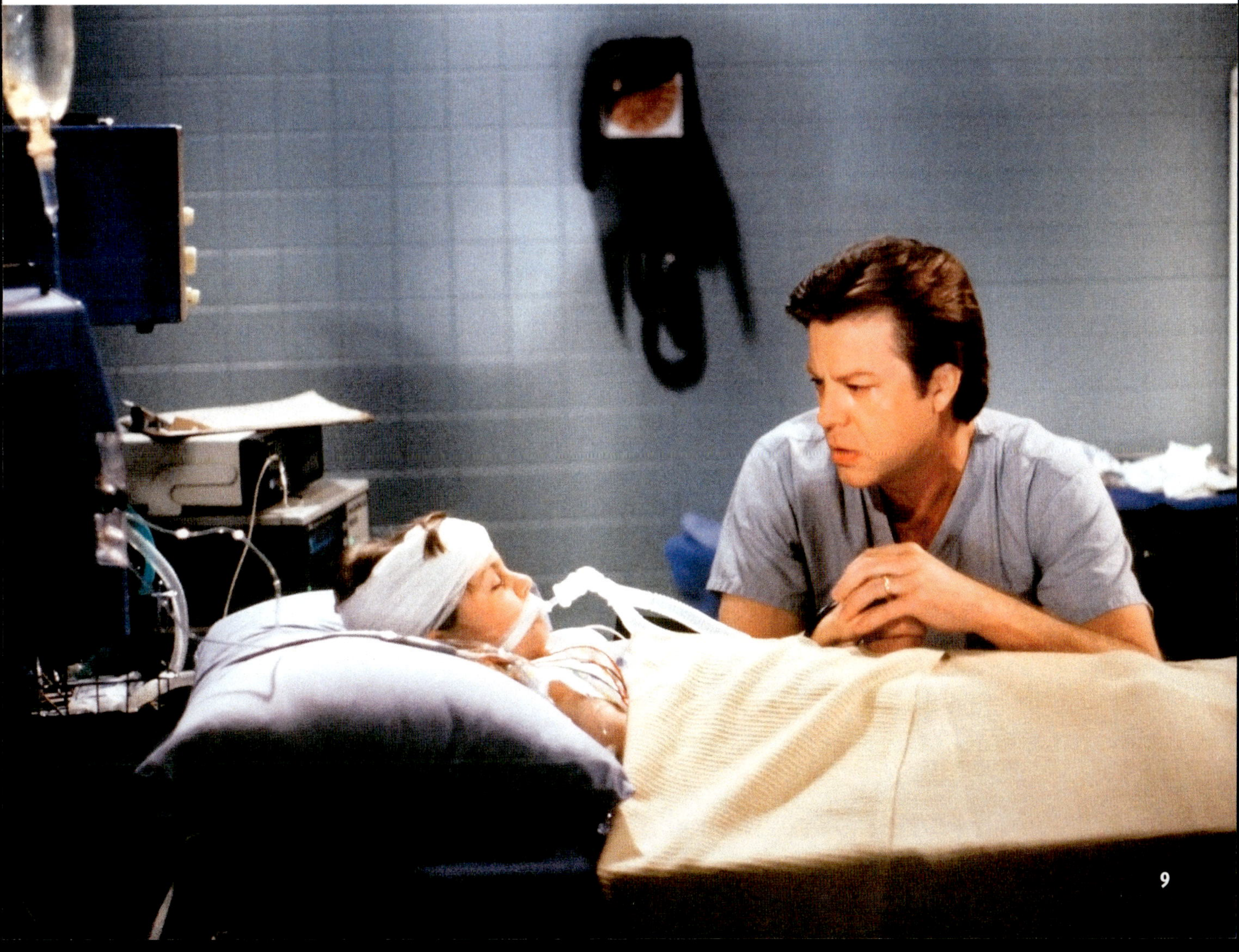

4

'CLINK-BOOM' (1996)

It was a devastating day for Sonny (Maurice Benard). His ex Brenda (Vanessa Marcil) wed Jax (Ingo Rademacher, above right, with Benard and Marcil) at the exact moment Sonny's pregnant wife, Lily (Lilly Melgar), died in a car bomb meant for Sonny. The episode is famously nicknamed "Clink-BOOM" in a nod to newlyweds Brenda and Jax clinking their champagne glasses as the camera cut to Lily turning (a tipsy) Sonny's keys to start his car, which then exploded (à la Michael Corleone's wife, Apollonia, in *The Godfather*). "*No!*" Sonny screamed as his car was engulfed in flames. Yes.

5

ALAN TRIES TO KILL RICK AND MONICA (1980)

Jealousy can make people do crazy things. Just ask Dr. Alan Quartermaine (Stuart Damon, right), who went crazy after his wife, Monica (Leslie Charleson), cheated on him with fellow doctor Rick Webber (Chris Robinson, left) and became pregnant. Blood tests led them to believe the baby was Rick's, so Alan set out to kill them both—unsuccessfully. Ultimately the baby turned out to be his and grew up to be A.J. (Alan Jr.) Quartermaine.

6

JASON LOSES HIS MEMORY (1995)

Who knew a head injury could turn a bright young med student into a Mob enforcer? That's what happened to Jason Quartermaine (Steve Burton) after he jumped into the passenger seat of A.J.'s car to stop his brother from driving drunk. A.J. (Sean Kanan, left, with Burton) hit a tree, and Jason was ejected. He woke up with no recollection of the past, but he knew enough to dislike most of his family. Jason dropped out of medical school and went to work for Sonny as a hit man. In a soap rarity, Jason never regained his memories.

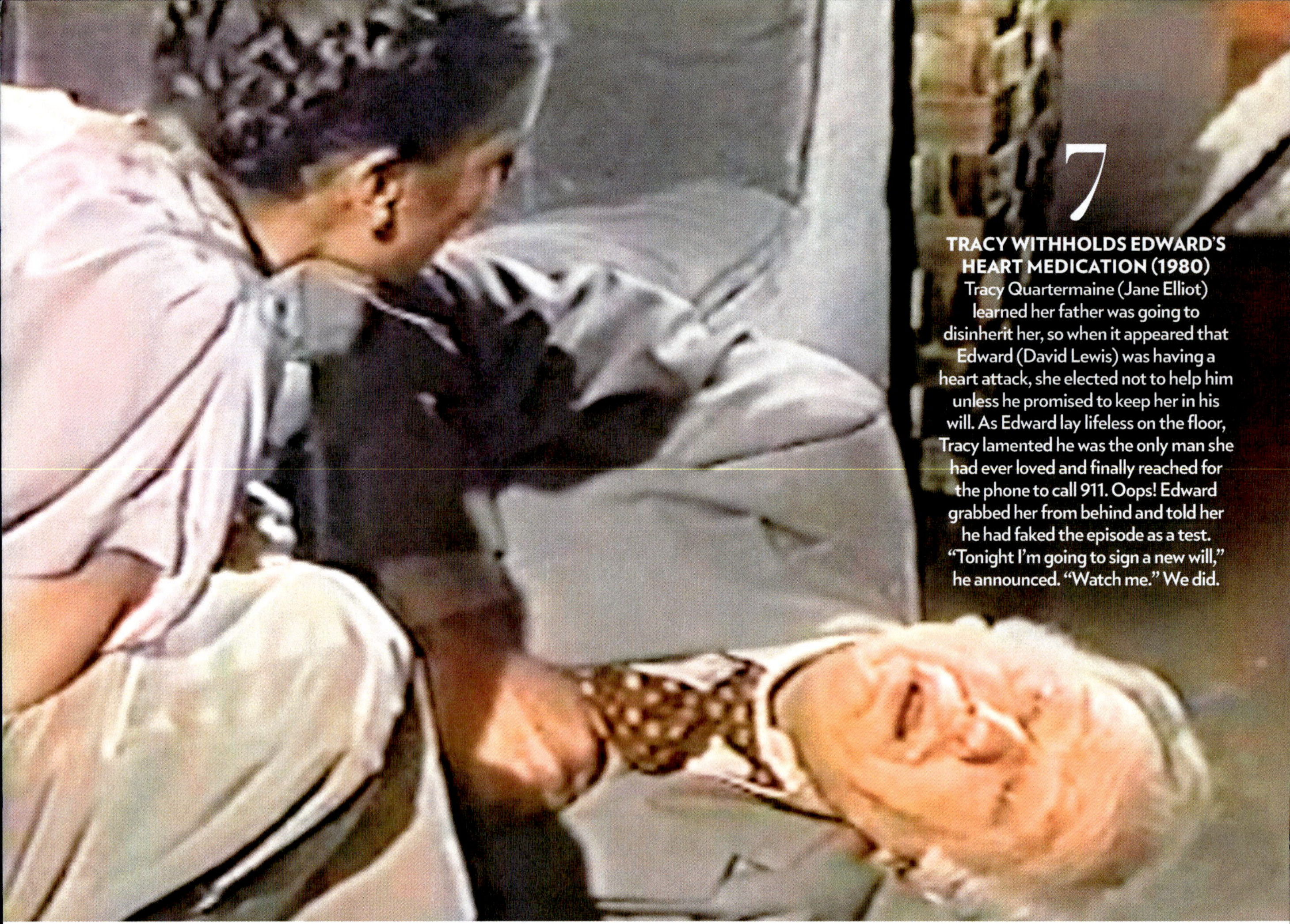

7

TRACY WITHHOLDS EDWARD'S HEART MEDICATION (1980)

Tracy Quartermaine (Jane Elliot) learned her father was going to disinherit her, so when it appeared that Edward (David Lewis) was having a heart attack, she elected not to help him unless he promised to keep her in his will. As Edward lay lifeless on the floor, Tracy lamented he was the only man she had ever loved and finally reached for the phone to call 911. Oops! Edward grabbed her from behind and told her he had faked the episode as a test. "Tonight I'm going to sign a new will," he announced. "Watch me." We did.

8

ANNA AND ROBERT HAVE A DAUGHTER! (1985)

Robin arrived in Port Charles with the last name Soltini, a grandmother named Filomena and a "family friend" called Anna (Finola Hughes) who she soon learned was her mother. When Anna's ex Robert (Tristan Rogers) met the 6-year-old, he did the math on her birth. "She captured my heart just like someone else did seven years ago," he deduced. "Robin Soltini. Should be Scorpio, shouldn't it?"

9

HEATHER FRAMES ANNE FOR MURDER (1981)

In an effort to win back her estranged husband, Jeff Webber, from his new love Anne Logan (Richard Dean Anderson and Susan Pratt, top), Heather (Robin Mattson, left) tried to get back Jeff's baby, whom she had secretly given birth to and sold on the black market. That made Diana Taylor (Brooke Bundy), who had adopted the boy, a target. Heather broke into Diana's house to kill her but found her already dead—so Heather wrote Anne's name in blood with Diana's hand to (literally) finger her for the crime. Heather's efforts to vanquish Anne from Jeff's life failed when Anne was exonerated and the real killer was revealed: It was Heather's mother, Alice Grant (Lieux Dressler)!

‘FELICIA AND ANNA WERE LOOKING OUT FOR OUR GIRL MAXIE’
—FINOLA HUGHES

10

FELICIA KILLS PETER AUGUST (2022)

After "dying" numerous times (most notably falling down the stairs during a fight with Finn and having his body hidden in the hospital freezer), Faison's evil son Peter (Wes Ramsey) was finally offed by Felicia (left) with a tire iron in an effort to protect her daughter Maxie. Anna came upon Peter's lifeless body (below) and, instead of calling 911, watched her nephew die. "The death of Peter was an extraordinary moment," Finola Hughes tells *People*. "Ultimately Anna didn't give the defining blow, but she sat there with him and didn't call the emergency team. She waited." So it's not murder when you're protecting a loved one?

THE ICONS
Dr. Steve Hardy (John Beradino) and dedicated (if love-cursed) nurse Jessie Brewer (Emily McLaughlin) were the heartbeat of *General Hospital* for years.

Drama on the *7th Floor*

THE '60s

IN THE SPRING OF 1963, ABC INTRODUCED VIEWERS TO A LIVELY HOSPITAL WHERE MEDICAL EMERGENCIES AND ROMANTIC ENTANGLEMENTS FILLED THE HOUR IN EQUAL MEASURE

INTENSIVE CARE
"Who wants to be alive with a face like this?" cried accident victim Angie Costello (Jana Taylor). "I wish I were dead!" She recovered, physically and spiritually, thanks to Dr. Hardy.

ON CALL
The *General Hospital* cast in 1966 (above).

MEDICAL SHOWS WERE HAVING a moment. *Dr. Kildare* and *Ben Casey* were prime-time hits. ABC's original concept for what became *General Hospital* wasn't a serial; instead, each day a policeman, a doctor and a nurse would encounter a problem and solve it during the episode. The network only shifted gears and created a more traditional serial when it became clear that another network also had a medical-themed soap opera in the works. In fact, ABC's *General Hospital* and NBC's *The Doctors* premiered on the very same day—Monday, April 1, 1963.

From the beginning, *GH* centered on the seventh floor of a hospital in an unnamed East Coast city (the locale wasn't designated Port Charles until the '70s) that seesawed wildly, and entertainingly, between medical emergencies—Lymphoma! Malaria! Murder by "Alkaloid X34"!—and the fraught romantic lives of doctors, nurses and even love- and lust-struck patients.

At the heart of it all were medico-with-a-heart-of-gold-and-a-chin-of-granite Dr. Steve Hardy (John Beradino, who would stay with the show until his death in 1996) and his best friend and devoted nurse, the unlucky-in-love Jessie Brewer (Emily McLaughlin). Fans longed for them to get together but had to settle for decades of vague sexual tension. And, alas, bad romantic choices on the part of Jessie, who *never* should have taken up with handsome, philandering Dr. Phil Brewer (first played by Roy Thinnes), seven years her junior. He dumped her for teacher Cynthia Allison ("I'm sorry I'm not as young and pretty as Cynthia!" Jessie cried). Then, missing Jessie, Dr. Phil got drunk and forced himself on her. For an encore, he had a secret affair with Polly, the scheming teenager who had gotten

STAYING POWER
Rachel Ames came aboard in 1964 as glamorous nurse Audrey March (opposite), the woman who could finally get Dr. Steve Hardy to stop thinking about work and even walk down the aisle. Through trial and tribulation—including divorce from Steve, two more marriages, an invalidated remarriage to Steve and a hostage crisis—Ames was a *GH* regular for nearly 40 years.

AUDREY (RACHEL AMES) APPEARED IN MORE THAN 900 EPISODES OF *GENERAL HOSPITAL*, FROM 1964 TO 2015

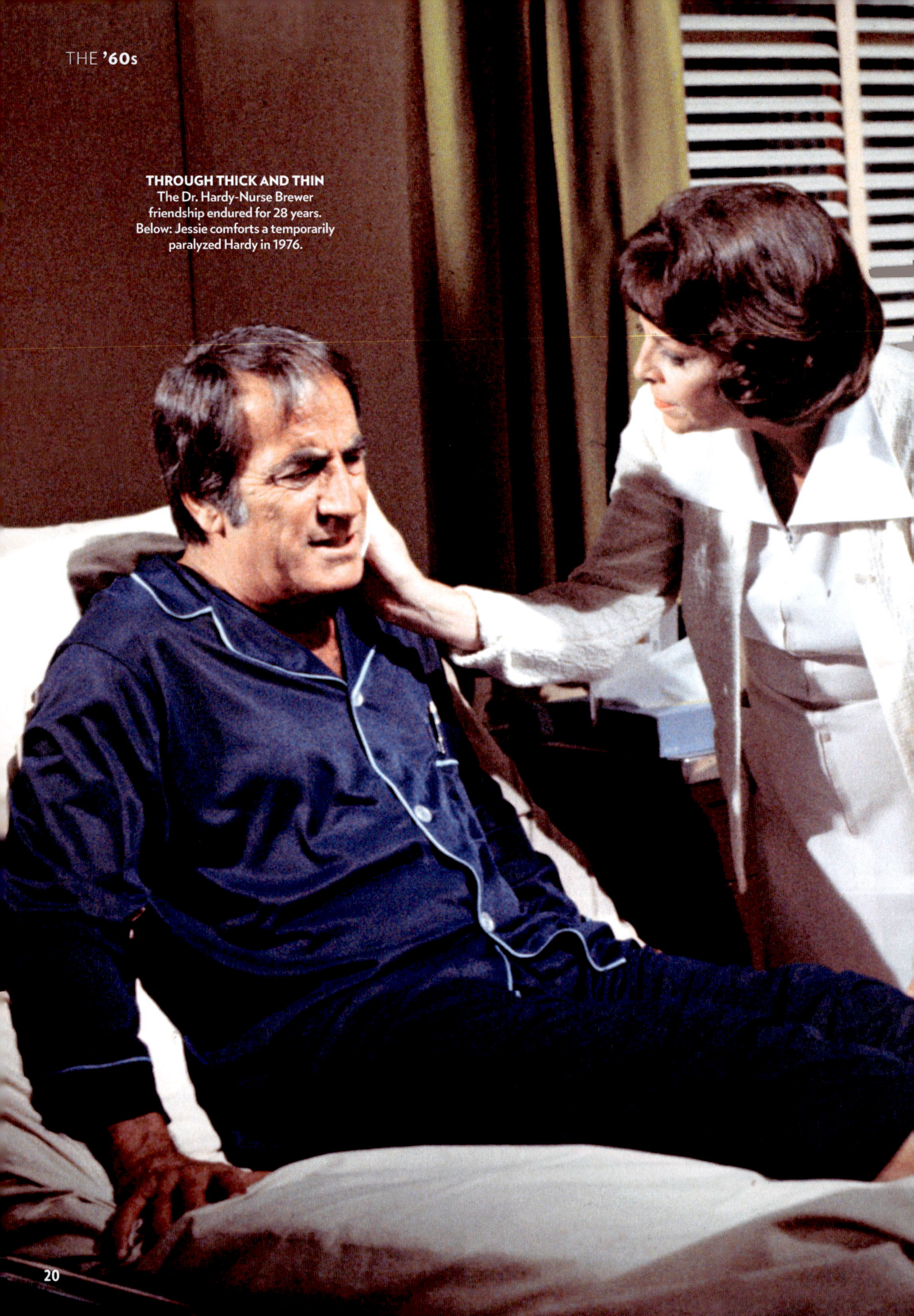

THROUGH THICK AND THIN
The Dr. Hardy-Nurse Brewer friendship endured for 28 years. Below: Jessie comforts a temporarily paralyzed Hardy in 1976.

Jessie convicted for a murder she did not commit! Despite all that, Jessie found it difficult to permanently drop-kick the hunk of human kryptonite out of her life.

Dr. Hardy, by contrast, initially seemed focused on everyone's life but his own; his first serious romantic interest, Peggy Mercer, sadly came to realize he was married to his job and ran off with a writer. Dr. Hardy eventually fell for globe-trotting nurse-flight attendant Audrey March (Rachel Ames), who thought there might be another, more passionate Steve Hardy lingering beneath that cool professional surface—"a real, living, exciting human being," as she put it, "a man, not just a doctor!"

"Audrey, you make me feel like I'm missing out on something," Steve replied. "I've never met anyone like you before!"

There were, of course, dramatic moments of romance thwarted, most notably when Audrey developed feelings for rich-but-malarial businessman Randy Washburn and told Dr. Hardy, "I don't consider myself good enough for you, Steve! The kind of woman you ought to marry is someone like Jessie!" Still, they eventually tied the knot, but this being a soap opera, things did not go smoothly: Dr. Hardy confronted evidence he was sterile ("I feel like a failure as a man!"), and after tragedy damaged their marriage, Audrey filed for divorce and left to work with orphans in Vietnam.

But romantic passion was never Dr. Hardy's trump suit; more than anything he was there to help the hopeless, as he did with teenage Angie Costello, who feared her beautiful young face—damaged in a car crash with her drunk boyfriend at the wheel, and still hidden in bandages—was forever scarred. "I don't want anybody to see my face!" she wailed. "Why don't you just leave the bandages on!"

"Angie, you can't hide behind those bandages forever!" Dr. Hardy replied. "Come back into the world again—live again!"

Angie later had to testify at her boyfriend's trial, but thanks to the unrelenting efforts of Dr. Hardy and Jessie, she looked great.

THE '70s

Young Doctors *in* Love

A NEW WAVE OF DOCTORS AND NURSES CHECKED IN, BRINGING A CONSTANT FLOW OF ROMANCE AND TURMOIL

ONCE AND AGAIN
As is common in Port Charles, Rick (Chris Robinson) and Lesley (Denise Alexander) were married, divorced, then remarried.

SOULMATES
Despite—or perhaps because of—all the drama, Monica (Leslie Charleson) and Alan (Stuart Damon) became one of daytime's most enduring duos.

SCHEMING SIBLINGS
Luke Spencer showed up in 1978 when his conniving sister Bobbie (Jacklyn Zeman) used him to try to get Scott (Kin Shriner, below, with Zeman) back from Laura.

LAURA 2.0
Genie Francis took over the role of Laura from Stacey Baldwin in 1977.

MURDER, SHE CLAIMED Lesley (right, with Monica) went to jail to protect her daughter Laura from a murder charge.

MOST OF THE '70S reinforced the Great Soap Opera Verities: (1) Anyone who dies off-camera will come back to life (Phil Brewer in a plane crash in South America, Rick Webber in a plane crash in Africa); (2) any sex you regret will, of course, lead to pregnancy (Lesley Faulkner, Jeff Webber with Heather); and (3) good news is frequently a bad omen (Dr. Steve Hardy, after discovering Audrey still loves him, falls down a flight of stairs and is paralyzed). And one more thing: that baby your wife is about to have?

Er, it's just maybe not yours.

Nurse Jessie continued her epic run of bad luck. Her romance with charming journalist Teddy Holmes came a cropper when he put her in debt and ran off with her 18-year-old niece. Then someone killed her ex Phil Brewer with a blunt instrument, and Jessie was (once again) jailed for a murder she did not commit. In the middle of the decade, Monica arrived to start messing, memorably, with anyone who came between her and Rick.

Dr. Monica Webber Quartermaine (first played by Patsy Rahn and later by Leslie Charleson) was the black heart of *GH* in the mid- to late '70s. She torpedoed her (outwardly) perfect marriage to Jeff Webber when his brother (also Monica's presumed dead former fiancé) Rick (Chris Robinson) turned up undead and she had an affair with him. Then she tried to derail Rick's upcoming marriage by blackmailing his fiancée Lesley (Denise Alexander)—which so upset her that she fell down the stairs and lost her baby. And when Rick and Lesley finally *did* get married, Monica slept with him again—after marrying handsome doctor Alan Quartermaine (Stuart Damon).

After a while, though, repetition began to pall; by 1978 ratings had dropped so far that *GH* was in danger of cancellation. ABC hired brash producer Gloria Monty to shake up the show; instead, she shook up the industry. Before long, *General Hospital* placed No. 1 in viewers for the first time, enjoying its highest ratings ever.

THE ORIGINALS
A pre-*MacGyver* Richard Dean Anderson (with Patsy Rahn, the first actress to play Monica) originated the role of Jeff in 1976.

MONEYMAKER
Monty (on-set with Geary in 1981) produced a quarter of ABC's profits during her heyday.

SPOTLIGHT

The Full Monty

General Hospital was sagging in the ratings in 1978 when ABC hired Gloria Monty as executive producer. Good move—in fact, perhaps one of the best in the history of daytime drama.

Petite and driven, Monty, who had previously directed the soaps *The Secret Storm* and *Bright Promise*, came in swinging: She hired younger actors, spiffed up the sets, jacked up the pace and introduced grittier and dicier plots—including Luke's rape of Laura. (Longtime star John Beradino may not have been joking when he complained of being pushed aside by young "freaks, creeps, pimps and hookers.") Monty ditched the safe confines of General Hospital's seventh floor and went on location—with unheard of story lines about evil plotters and magical Makuthian swords.

The results would prove remarkable, but the process was wrenching. "Gloria would crack the whip," recalls Brian Patrick Clarke, who played Grant Putnam. "You never knew which Gloria you were going to get." Says Leslie Charleson (Monica): "I'm sure [the stories] are all true. There were a lot of actors that went screaming out of the business in tears." Head writer Patricia Falken Smith, who quit along with six other scribes, felt more strongly, describing Monty as "a genius who runs a Gestapo operation."

But Monty saved the show. "She was a force of nature, a tiny woman who was an enormous talent," says Anthony Geary (Luke).

She was also a gold mine. Three years after her arrival, *GH* was earning $50 million a year—about double the profit of the far-more-expensive-to-produce nighttime soap *Dallas*. Monty left in 1987, but when *GH*'s ratings fell, ABC brought her back in 1990. She failed to recapture the old magic—bringing Geary back as Luke's lookalike blue-collar cousin Bill Eckert flopped—and left after two years. But the revolution she sparked changed soaps ever after.

TROPHY TIME
GH was nominated for Outstanding Drama Series at the Daytime Emmys every year between 1981 and 1986, winning twice ('81 and '84).

'70s SUPER-COUPLES

FLEETING LOVE
Laura and Scotty were married in 1979, but thanks to Luke, it would not be happily ever after for the couple.

POWER PAIR
When not busy dealing with the antics of everyone else in town, psychiatrist Gail Adamson (Susan Brown) and lawyer Lee Baldwin (Peter Hansen) found time for love and eventually were married.

SECRETS AND LIES
Heather (Mary O'Brien) manipulated Jeff (Richard Dean Anderson) into a relationship.

One generation of the lustful, conniving and lovelorn fades and another arrives; but *General Hospital* abides forever. So it was in the 1970s, when the focus of story lines and bloodlines shifted from Dr. Steve Hardy to his out-of-wedlock son Jeff Webber and Jeff's half brother Dr. Rick Webber. Enter gorgeous intern Monica Bard Webber, and much begetting, lying with and lying to ensued. She had married Jeff after her fiancé Rick was killed in Africa, only to cause major marital difficulties when Rick turned up undead. Thanks to Jeff's rebound marriage to conniving Heather Grant and Rick's hookup with pregnant widow Lesley Faulkner (soon-to-be Webber), things got even more complicated.

By decade's end Lesley's long-lost daughter Laura had grown into a beautiful young killer—she accidentally killed her older lover after he scorned her. Laura wed handsome Scotty Baldwin, whose ex, bad girl Bobbie Spencer (Jacklyn Zeman), then enlisted her thuggy brother Luke (newcomer Anthony Geary) in a series of nasty plots intended to undo the pair. When Luke found himself falling for wholesome, fresh-faced Laura and she thrilled to his edgy presence, the stage was set for *GH*'s most intoxicating coupling of all. But viewers were left with an unsettling cliff-hanger when Luke and Laura's first passionate embrace went way, way over the line.

WHO'S YOUR DADDY?
At the christening of her son A.J., Monica (in pink) wasn't sure if the father was her husband (by her side) or her old flame Rick (far left).

THE SHOW TOOK SOME OF ITS BIGGEST SWINGS, OFTEN VENTURING FAR BEYOND PORT CHARLES AND, OF COURSE, SHOWCASING DAYTIME'S MOST ELECTRIFYING COUPLE

THE '80s

Remaking *the* Rules

CLIMATE CHANGE
Some purists scoffed at new wild plots like the hunt for the Ice Princess (with, from left, Scorpio, Laura and Luke) and the Aztec treasure, but ratings climbed. Said Geary: "Pretty soon every other show was freezing the planet too."

SNOW DAYS
Above: After a quarrel with Holly, Luke—who had briefly been the mayor of Port Charles—went camping in the mountains and was buried in an avalanche in 1983.

CLIFF-HANGER
Opposite: In a scene shot on location on Catalina Island, Calif., in 1986, Kevin (Kevin Bernhardt) tried to kill his wife, Terry (Robyn Bernard), but instead went over the cliff himself.

CALL IT ALCHEMY, CALL IT HARMONIC convergence. But don't call it predictable: Whatever happened to *General Hospital* in the early '80s—some once-in-a-lifetime combination of Gloria Monty's fevered vision, Luke and Laura's dynamic chemistry and a sudden, unquenchable American appetite for romantic fantasy—produced a daytime phenomenon unseen before or since.

Luke and Laura's summer on the run—pursued by not one, but two hit men, one in drag—drew legions of fans and eventually led to their Nov. 16-17, 1981, wedding, days that will live forever in soap history. (The landmark event remains the most-watched daytime event of all time.) Still, although it was the biggest *General Hospital* event of the '80s, it was far from the decade's only hallmark. Breaking free of the constraints of medical drama, Monty introduced wild plots, chief among them a scheme by Mikkos Cassadine (John Colicos) to freeze Port Charles and everyone in it, like a giant Popsicle. Luke saved the city, and the world, by typing a secret code into a computer at the last possible second.

Indeed, the '80s marked a turning point for the show—and eventually all soaps. Plots shifted from love, lust and hospital emergencies to wild sci-fi fantasies involving the Ice Princess (a massive uncut diamond containing the secret formula for Earth-freezing carbonic snow, enabling megalomaniac Mikkos to boast, "The entire world will live by my rule! I will be in supreme command!"). There was also the Sword of Malkuth (needed by the mysterious David Grey to help overthrow a

'IT WAS REALLY THE HIGH POINT OF *GENERAL HOSPITAL* AS FAR AS I'M CONCERNED. WE WERE BREAKING THE MOLD'
—ANTHONY GEARY, TO *ENTERTAINMENT WEEKLY*, IN 2008

UNDER ATTACK
In 1987 the DVX, a nefarious KGB-like group, seized *General Hospital* and poisoned Bobbie (left) with a virus that left her paralyzed.

faraway kingdom); the Prometheus Disc (a top-secret energy source sought by a notorious international espionage organization, the DVX); and an Aztec treasure (Frisco's ring was a key to a secret vault; Luke, in pursuit of the loot, was framed for murder). By comparison, another '80s plotline—the Secret of L'Orleans, involving a long-ago murder and a nun with amnesia—seemed positively quaint.

Monty didn't give up on creating supercouples and compelling characters, including, notably, dashing secret agent posing as a playboy-financier Robert Scorpio (Tristan Rogers), who over the course of the decade pulled a gun on Luke, got knocked unconscious by Luke, became Luke's best friend and—after Luke disappeared in an avalanche—married Luke's pregnant girlfriend Holly (Emma Samms) so she could stay in the country. "Gloria gave us the kind of freedom that no longer exists in the genre," Anthony Geary noted when Monty died in 2006. "It was a time when decisions were not made by committee."

STONE COLD
The mysterious Ice Princess (right) was an uncut diamond painted black to conceal its true power—to freeze the world.

SCHEME QUEEN
Above: The devious Tracy Quartermaine (Jane Elliot) has long been a troublemaker in Port Charles.

DEVIL DOG
Above, right: Grant Putnam (Brian Patrick Clarke) kidnapped Anna, with help from his guard dog Satan.

'80s SUPER-COUPLES

Sure, Luke and Laura were the decade's supercouple icons, but they weren't *GH*'s only red-hot romance. At least three other delicious duos kept viewers tuning in:

Aztec princess and amnesia victim Felicia Cummings (Kristina Malandro, later Wagner) and her dream lover, rock singer Frisco Jones (Jack Wagner), met cute, Shakespeare-style, when he caught her, disguised as a boy, trying to steal a ring from his bedroom. His death caused her much heartache; his sudden reappearance a year later, merely caused her to faint.

The passion of Robert (Tristan Rogers) and Holly Scorpio (Emma Samms) survived all adversity, including the reappearance of her ex-love Luke Spencer, whom she had mourned after his apparent death in an avalanche *and* the sudden appearance of Robert's ex-wife Anna Devane (Finola Hughes), with a secret daughter in tow. Holly and Robert's love ended only when she died—completely and, it seemed, irrevocably—in a plane crash. Robert, devastated, eventually found himself again drawn to Anna Devane.

Too late! Devane, a onetime villain turned Port Charles's police chief, was now betrothed to the hottest guy in town, the dangerous but dashing Duke Lavery (Ian Buchanan), a Mobbed-up Scotsman with a seductive brogue. They kept their illicit love under the covers as best they could, but once the gangster and his police moll made a steaming hot spectacle of themselves on the dance floor at Duke's nightclub, all of Port Charles learned what viewers had known all along—these two were hot for each other.

HOT TO TROT
Anna and Duke were more than dance partners

TILL DEATH
Holly and Robert stayed together until her apparent demise in 1987.

BACK FROM BEYOND
Felicia and Frisco were reunited in 1989—in the town's catacombs.

WEDDING DAZE
"I never realized how big it was when it was happening, and I'm constantly amazed, as the years go by…that people still care," Francis (with Geary) said in 2006.

LUKE & LAURA

The Dynamic Duo

In 1981 a once-in-the-history-of-soaps convergence of story, character, a wild cameo from Elizabeth Taylor, and national appetite turned the wedding of two *General Hospital* characters, Luke and Laura, into a cultural milestone—and the highest-rated moment in daytime history, with 30 million tuning in. (Taylor, a rabid fan, had volunteered to crash the wedding as Helena Cassadine and put a curse on the couple. "I'm wild about that show," the Hollywood icon said. "I had a ball!")

How big was it? Magazines, including *People,* put Luke and Laura on the covers. Bars and college dorms threw viewing parties. A song called "General Hospi-Tale" became a Top 40 hit. The episode also minted new fans, including the Kansas City Royals baseball team, which came by the Los Angeles set for a tour.

The draw was two unique characters and a plotting and pacing new to soap operas. Lucas Lorenzo Spencer, played by Anthony Geary, originally appeared as a low-level Mob hit man in what was supposed to be a short-term role. Laura Webber (Genie Francis) grew up torn between her adoptive and biological mothers until accidentally killing her older lover David Hamilton as a teen. Mom Lesley took the rap, Laura married sweet Scotty Baldwin (Kin Shriner), and her future looked bright.

Enter Luke and the soap's most controversial story line to this day: a romance that began with a rape. The set-up seemed innocent enough: Luke managed the Campus Disco, where Laura was a waitress, and they developed a flirty friendship in 1979. One night, thinking his latest assignment from the Mob was about to get him killed, Luke drank heavily and confessed his love to Laura. "I'm not going to die without holding you in my arms just one time. Dance with me." As they swayed to Herb Alpert's "Rise," Laura grew fearful and tried to leave. The camera panned away as Luke forced himself on her and

1. WEDDING CRASHER
Scotty prepares to catch the bouquet from his ex-wife—and quickly starts catching Luke's punches.

2. ON THE RUN
The couple spent the summer and fall of 1981 on an adventure to save the world.

3. WHERE IT ALL STARTED
Luke and Laura met at the Campus Disco, scene of his fateful assault of her.

4. FOUNTAIN OF TRUTH
The Left-Handed Boy turned out to be a statue—which held the key to decode Frank Smith's incriminating black book.

5. A DAY OF DRAMA
Luke comforted Laura after his over-the-top wedding-day brawl with Scotty.

6. THEME SONG
"Think of Laura," Christopher Cross's tribute to a college student's tragic death, was co-opted by *GH* and hit the Top 10 in 1984.

2

3

5

4

FAMILY PORTRAIT
Their marriage didn't last, but Luke and Laura's legacy includes son Lucky (Jonathan Jackson) and daughter Lulu.

Homemakers find a feisty new ally: Betty Friedan

NOVEMBER 16, 1981 • 95¢

People weekly

On the job with the top cancer doc

Shy Di wows Wales

Joan Collins: her agonizing vigil

Liz & Luke & Laura

An advance peek at TV's wedding of the year (and look who's crashing)

General Hospital's Anthony Geary and Genie Francis—with guest star Elizabeth Taylor

COVER WHIRL
"I remember it going very quickly," Francis says of the *People* photo shoot with Taylor in '81. "Everything that involved Elizabeth had a sort of protocol attached, almost like royalty."

BACK TO THE CHAPEL
The pair reunited—and were remarried—in 2006, a quarter century after their first wedding.

Laura screamed, "No!" After it was over, Laura ran sobbing out of the disco, and Luke cried, "What have I done?"

The aftermath was murky at best. The producers, who were planning to kill Luke, noted the piles of fan mail coming into the studio for the couple and began referring to the act as a "seduction." Laura refused to name her attacker and gradually admitted she had feelings for Luke—and that maybe, perhaps it wasn't exactly rape.

The reversal was head-spinning. But Geary and Francis had amazing chemistry, and fans just wanted to see them together. Interest exploded in 1980 when Luke and Laura went on the run, providing a daily dose of high adventure (searching for the Left-Handed Boy statue, dodging a cross-dressing hit man, getting trapped in a department store for the night, then re-creating the "Walls of Jericho" scene from *It Happened One Night* in their hotel room). Teens and college students tuned in by the millions—a new audience that thrilled advertisers. What was the draw? "Luke's a guy with bad qualities, but he's also sensitive and romantic," Geary told *Newsweek*. "People root for him." Noted Francis, who was 14 when she first appeared on *General Hospital* in 1977: "The best way [to draw younger viewers] was to give them one of their peers, and that was me. We did a first-love story with real-life sex, romance and heartbreak. It's every teenager's story."

By the time of the wedding, Luke had saved Laura—and the world!—by defeating the evil Cassadines. On Nov. 17, 1981, Luke and Laura said "I do." When Laura tossed her bouquet, it was caught by her long-lost husband Scotty, the only one who could contest her quickie Mexican divorce. Luke leaped over the balcony, punched Scotty, and the wedding stood.

Their happily ever after was challenged, of course. Francis, bone-tired, left the show early the next year. "I'm 19, I've been on since I was 14, and I'm absolutely exhausted," she said. Geary echoed the sentiment but stayed. "I have given my life to this show—physically, emotionally, spiritually," he said. "Genie and I have carried as much as 60 pages of dialogue a day, four or five days a week. No nighttime show, no film makes those demands." Two years later Francis rejoined the show long enough to help wrap up loose ends for Geary's departure: After the couple's happy reunion at Luke's mayoral inauguration (Laura had found her way back after being kidnapped by—and forced to marry—Stavros Cassadine), they enjoyed a brief stint as Port Charles's First Couple before growing restless and deciding to go see the world. They reappeared in the 1990s with a son and shortly after gave birth to a daughter. At the decade's end, *GH* revisited the "seduction" for what is was when Lucky Spencer learned his father had raped his mother. "The times are different," explained Wendy Riche, executive producer at the time. "What the audience perceives and what they expect is very different from what it was 20 years ago. They are more conscious date rape is unacceptable."

GH celebrated the couple's 25th anniversary in 2006 by marrying them again, even if it was invalid because of Luke's marriage to Tracy Quartermaine (Jane Elliot). Luke was presumed dead in a 2022 cable-car crash (possibly orchestrated by his old nemesis Victor Cassadine). Laura tied the knot with Dr. Kevin Collins (Jon Lindstrom) in 2017 and remains the heart of the show as mayor of Port Charles. Will Luke ever turn up alive? As they say in the soaps biz, stay tuned.

THE '90s

Back to (Soapy) Reality

SCI-FI FADES, SOCIAL ISSUES STEP TO THE FORE, AND—WHO ELSE?—LUKE AND LAURA COME BARRELING BACK INTO PORT CHARLES IN A BIG PINK CADILLAC

WEDDING CRASHER
Ryan attacked Felicia, preventing her from marrying Mac in 1994. She and Mac ultimately did tie the knot in 1998.

‘IT WAS A FUN ENTRANCE. I LOVED A LOT ABOUT THAT STORY. WE DID ACTUALLY GET IN THAT RIVER. MAN, THAT WAS COLD!’

—GENIE FRANCIS, ON LUKE & LAURA’S SPLASHY RETURN

ITH THE VERY NOTABLE exception of Casey the Alien (he came to Earth, and Port Charles specifically, to retrieve crystals from his home planet, Lumina), the 1990s marked a shift away from fantasy and toward social issues. The usual romantic and criminal mayhem—the bomb in the hockey puck, the bomb in the wedding bouquet, the evil Faison (Anders Hove) using mind control to get Anna to spy on Scorpio—continued, but *General Hospital* also explored, through the lives of its characters, alcoholism, drug addiction, child molestation and, in very memorable story lines, breast cancer and AIDS.

Indeed, one of the decade’s least sudsy story lines proved an all-time weeper. After playing Shakespeare’s iconic star-crossed teen lovers at the Nurses’ Ball, Stone Cates (Michael Sutton) and Robin Scorpio (Kimberly McCullough) suffered their own tragedy in 1995, when Stone was diagnosed with HIV and later died of AIDS. Sutton was nominated for a Daytime Emmy for his portrayal, and McCullough won one for her role as the surviving girlfriend who struggled with the emotional and physical toll of her own infection. Both the American Red Cross and the Ryan White Foundation praised the show for raising public

THEY’RE BACK!
Above: Luke and Laura took a train, plane and helicopter and parachuted into a river (above) to get back to Port Charles. The scene was filmed near Rochester, N.Y.

THE KIDS ARE ALL RIGHT
Opposite: The new youth movement included (left to right) Steve Burton (Jason), Vanessa Marcil (Brenda), Sean Kanan (A.J.), Antonio Sabàto Jr. (Jagger), Cari Shayne (Karen) and Kimberly McCullough (Robin).

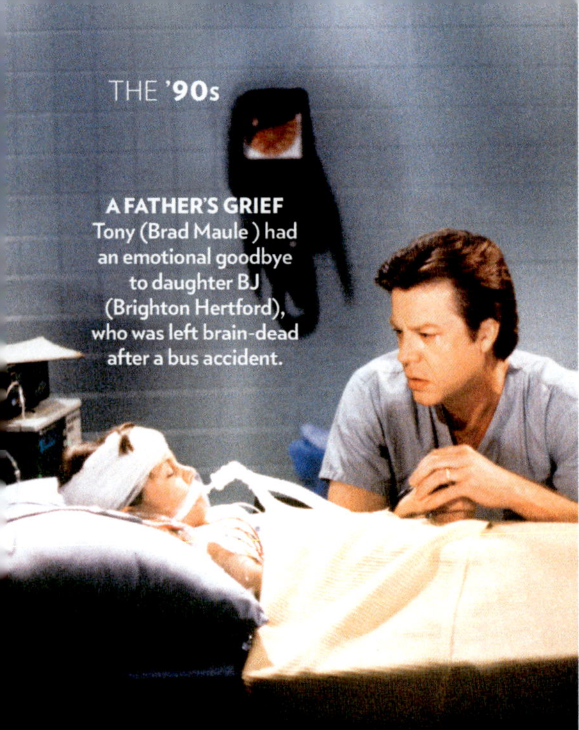

A FATHER'S GRIEF Tony (Brad Maule) had an emotional goodbye to daughter BJ (Brighton Hertford), who was left brain-dead after a bus accident.

PUPPY LOVE Luke and Laura's dog Foster (left) ran off with Edward Quartermaine's pooch Annabelle (right), and they had a pup, Raoul.

LOVE INTERRUPTED The romance of Stone and Robin came to a devastating end when he died of AIDS.

awareness and for tackling issues, including safe sex and the dangers of prenatal infection.

Of course, there were some of the usual only-in-Port Charles moments, including when Ryan (Jon Lindstrom) crashed the wedding of Felicia and Mac Scorpio (John J. York) with a bomb. And, in a strange twist, Anthony Geary came back to the show but initially played Luke's lookalike blue-collar cousin Bill Eckert. When that failed to capture audiences, the writers brought back Luke and killed off Bill—who died in Luke's arms. "Bitter justice," said Bill, staring into Luke's eyes, "the last face I see is my own."

That set the stage for the 1993 return of Luke and Laura. On the run from murderous mobster Frank Smith (Mitchell Ryan), they had been happily, anonymously running a diner in Canada. But a bomb in their truck let them know Smith was onto them, so they decided to return to Port Charles intent on destroying Smith once and for all. After that things got really complicated. As Laura said to Luke, "With Tiffany following Sean following you following me following Frank Smith, it's beginning to look like a conga line!"

We also met Brooklyn native Sonny Corinthos (Maurice Benard) in 1993, who ran the Paradise Lounge for Frank Smith, where high school student Karen Wexler (Scotty's daughter) worked as a stripper. Sonny teamed up with Luke to put an end to Smith, then claimed his place as Mob boss, where he has remained ever since.

SWAYING FOR A CAUSE The 1995 event featured a colorful performance by (from left) Joseph C. Phillips (Justus Ward), Jonathan Jackson, Anthony Geary and Rosalind Cash (Mary Mae Ward).

SPOTLIGHT

Nurses' Ball

Escapism seldom looks as good as when the residents of Port Charles get together to put on their annual show-within-the-show. The Nurses' Ball, first staged as an AIDS fundraiser in 1994, became a '90s fixture and allowed *General Hospital* stars to sing, dance and strut their characters' (and their own) hidden talents.

GH was one of the first soaps to shine the light of daytime TV on a health disaster that even many prime-time shows had failed to address. Still, the message never overwhelmed the entertainment, which often ended with a wardrobe malfunction that left emcee Lucy Coe (Lynn Herring)strutting her stuff in her skivvies.

After more than a decade's absence, the Nurses' Ball returned in 2013—including a performance of "Jessie's Girl" by Rick Springfield (as himself)—and has once again become a highly anticipated annual tradition in Port Charles.

'90s SUPER-COUPLES

There may be no aphrodisiac like a brush with death. And when it comes on the heels of a speedboat chase in the Caribbean that nearly sent Sonny and Brenda (Maurice Benard and Vanessa Marcil) from here to eternity in 1994, *GH*'s first couple re-created Burt Lancaster and Deborah Kerr's famous sand, sea and sex scene.

Nineties pop culture—rave parties and strip clubs—figured into the steamy story line that began with the 1993 Valentine's Day hookup of Jagger Cates (Antonio Sabàto Jr.) and Karen Wexler (Cari Shayne). The couple survived Karen's tripping and stripping, and their love grew stronger.

Ned Ashton (Wally Kurth) led a double life as a rock singer named Eddie Maine and fell for band manager Lois Cerullo (Rena Sofer). A little hiccup (bigamy, on his part) did cause turbulence in their marriage—but that was nothing a surprise pregnancy couldn't solve. As for the two-timing Ned/Eddie's other wife, Katherine Bell (Mary Beth Evans): The news only got worse. Stefan Cassadine (Stephen Nichols) accidentally shot her, paralyzing her, then asked her to marry him. Sadly their engagement party was ruined when she fell to her (apparent) death from a parapet. Later, after becoming engaged to Stefan's nephew (who she thought was his son) Nikolas Cassadine (Tyler Christopher), she was pushed from the same parapet, this time with a more permanent result.

MAKING MUSIC TOGETHER
Above: When Lois found out her rock star husband had been hiding his true identity (and another wife), Ned had to win her over with romance and roller coasters.

REUNITED
Left: As Stefan and Katherine, Stephen Nichols and Mary Beth Evans re-created their chemistry from *Days of Our Lives*.

UNFAITHFULLY YOURS
Jagger and Karen worked hard to improve their lives, but their marriage was ultimately doomed by his infidelity.

'THEY ARE BOTH SO DYSFUNCTIONAL AND DAMAGED IN A CERTAIN WAY THAT ONLY EACH OTHER COULD REALLY ACCEPT THE OTHER PERSON'

—VANESSA MARCIL, TO *ENTERTAINMENT WEEKLY*, IN 2011

MEANT FOR EACH OTHER Brenda and Sonny fell in love immediately, but it took nearly two decades before they finally wed.

THE '00s Crime Wave

FOR MOST OF THE DECADE, THE SHOW WAS MARRIED TO THE MOB. MURDER, MAYHEM AND OTHER ASSORTED CRISES PLAGUED PORT CHARLES

FATHER KNOWS BEST
Edward (left) was always warning his family (including Alan, Monica, Skye and Ned) about the Mob.

CLOSE CALL
With Liz and Jason at her bedside, Sam (Kelly Monaco) eventually recovered after being shot by her lover's rival.

ESCAPE PLAN
Carly and Alexis attempted to flee a fire at the Port Charles Hotel.

UNLUCKY SHOT After firing at a rival, Sonny realized that he actually hit Carly—as she was giving birth to their son Morgan.

GENERAL HOSPITAL in the 2000s could have been retitled *It's Always Sonny in Port Charles*. Maurice Benard's tormented mobster-with-a-soul dominated the show; rare was the day Sonny wasn't being shot at, stabbed, bombed or doing unto others in similar fashion. Sonny hung A.J. on a meat hook; accidentally shot his own wife, Carly (Tamara Braun), while she was giving birth; and plugged an unarmed cop—only to discover it was his own son Dante (Dominic Zamprogna).

Of course, bad things have always happened in Port Charles, but this decade in particular offered a cavalcade of calamity. For starters, tourists would be well-advised to avoid the Metro Court Hotel, which got its name after a 2004 fire when Jax (Ingo Rademacher) bought the place and renamed it for his then-fiancée, Courtney (sister of his archenemy Sonny). Next up: Jax's brother Jerry held half the town hostage there in 2007, resulting in a deadly explosion. You might want to be careful about your mode of transport too: A 2005 train

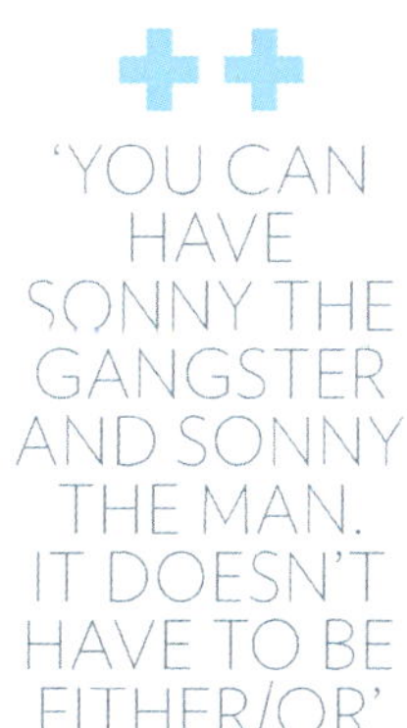

'YOU CAN HAVE SONNY THE GANGSTER AND SONNY THE MAN. IT DOESN'T HAVE TO BE EITHER/OR'

—MAURICE BENARD, TO *TV INSIDER*, IN 2016

FAREWELL, ALAN
Emily (Natalia Livingston) sat with her father, Alan (Stuart Damon), when he suffered a heart attack during the Metro Court crisis in 2007. He died later after surgery.

wreck left many of Port Charles's finest trapped in a tunnel. A night out wasn't safe either: At 2007's dressy Black & White Ball, a blackout provided cover for not one but two homicidal maniacs, who between them caused Port Charles's population—historically subject to sudden fluctuation—to drop again.

Also, things in Port Charles tended to explode with impressive frequency. Jax's car blew up in 2007; soon after, Sonny's limo did the same, and his warehouses were blown up in 2004 and a ship in 2009.

And, of course, it wouldn't be *General Hospital* without a little Luke and Laura. The pair reunited in the early part of the decade to search for their son Lucky (Jonathan Jackson), feared dead. He was alive but had been kidnapped and brainwashed by Helena Cassadine and Cesar Faison. Unluckily for Luke, once Lucky was safe, Laura left town again.

Then in 2006, after Laura awakened from a catatonic state (which was triggered when she regained her memories of accidentally killing a woman in self-defense as a teenager), she and Luke remarried on their 25th-wedding anniversary. Tracy (Jane Elliot), to whom Luke was also apparently married at the time, got drunk and had to be removed from the wedding. Later, the drug that had revived Laura wore off, and she returned to catatonia.

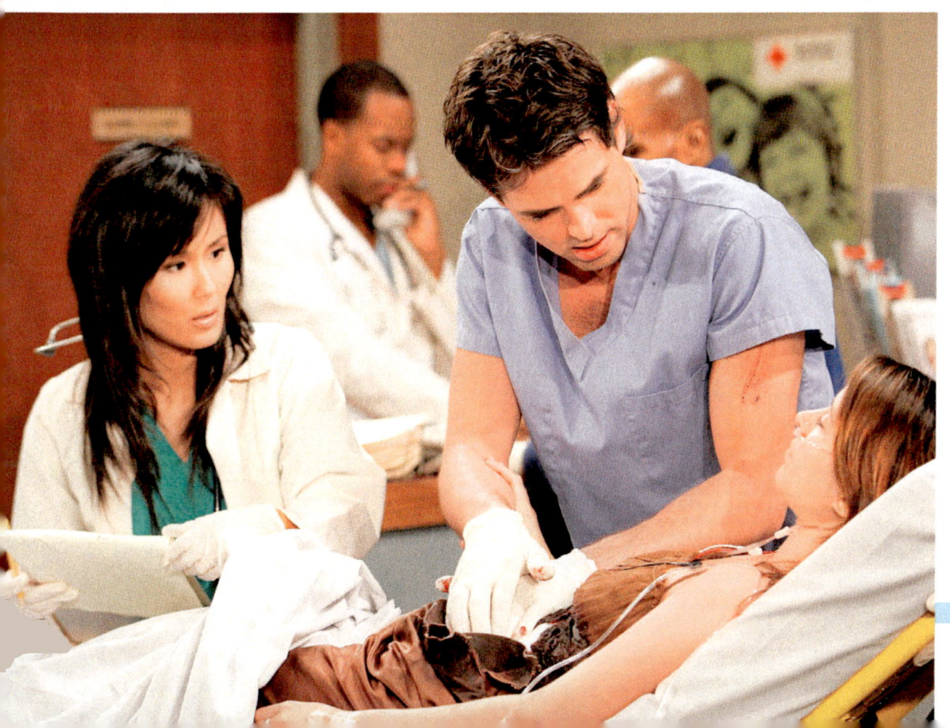

CONSTANT CHAOS
Above, left: Emily was at the center of tragedies like the attack on the Black & White Ball (with Nikolas).

OUT OF THE WRECKAGE
Above, right: Sonny and Emily helped a pregnant Alexis after a train collision.

TO THE RESCUE
Left: Kelly (Minae Noji) and Patrick (Jason Thompson) saved Robin after the Metro Court massacre.

THE GREAT DEBATE
Jason found love with both Liz (right) and Sam (below), igniting one of the most passionate social media *GH* debates of the decade: Liason or JaSam? He has a son with each partner and cared for them long after their dramatic breakups.

ON AND OFF
Maxie and Spinelli almost got married but eventually ended up as friends.

HITTING THE SHEETS
After months of will-they-or-won't-they tension, Lulu and Dante finally sealed the deal.

READY FOR PRIME TIME
Robin and Patrick's relationship took center stage in the nighttime spinoff *General Hospital: Night Shift*.

'00s SUPER-COUPLES

Love on *General Hospital* is never a walk in the park; it's more like running hurdles or a gauntlet that lovers must overcome.

Dante and Lulu survived, among other things, the revelation that he was an undercover cop; his getting shot by Sonny, who turned out to be his dad; and Lulu's brief stint in a bordello (she was only a waitress). Jason and Sam (aka "JaSam") (briefly) survived his risky surgery, her sleeping with her stepdad and his passionate affair with Liz that resulted in a child, Jake. Spinelli and Maxie ("Spixie") overcame her past (man stealer, drug supplier, thief) and his predilection for helping mobsters, but they eventually split. But the Most Challenged Couple Award probably belongs to Patrick and Robin, who met for the first time as he was having sex with a nurse at the hospital. Since then they've survived his HIV scare; her getting shot during the Metro Court hostage crisis; his psycho ex Dr. Lisa Niles; and Robin being kidnapped and left in the bottom of a well.

2010 TO TODAY

Love Actually

ROMANCE HAS COME ROARING BACK, THOUGH NOT EVERYONE IS LIVING HAPPILY EVER AFTER. THIS IS PORT CHARLES, AFTER ALL!

PICTURE-PERFECT
Morgan tried to freeze time with this 2015 selfie of the extended Corinthos family. From left: Dante, his son Rocco, Lulu (partially hidden), Morgan's then-girlfriend Kiki, Carly, Sonny, Avery, Kristina and Michael.

IOLENCE TOOK a back seat to love after the aughts. But for every happy event (Sonny marrying Brenda in 2011) there seemed to be a sad one (Liz and Jason's son Jake dying that same year). Jake was revealed to be alive in 2015 having been held captive by—who else?—Helena Cassadine (played since 1997 by Constance Towers), but other core characters didn't fare as well. The Quartermaines said goodbye to Edward and A.J.; Sonny mourned his son Morgan and his father, Mike; Ava buried daughter Kiki; Liz lost hubby Franco, and Maxie bid farewell to Nathan by placing a sonogram of their unborn child on his casket. Sniff!

If any one character embodied all that kissing (and killing), it was Jason Morgan (Steve Burton). He romanced Sam (Kelly Monaco) and Liz (Rebecca Herbst) with equal gusto, which was impressive considering that he died in 2012. Jason came back to Port Charles with amnesia in 2014 thinking he was Drew Cain (now played by Billy Miller) and returned for real in 2017 (with Burton back in the role and Drew rewritten as Jason's twin in another only-in-soaps move) and then died again in 2021.

The increased use of social media also advanced "squish names" in the soaps zeitgeist (think Bennifer!) for the most popular couples. Jason's partnerships were dubbed Jasam and Liason, while other duos included Julexis (Julian and Alexis), CarSon (Carly and Sonny), Nava (Nikolas and Ava) and Vanna (Valentin and Anna), all the way up to current sweeties Spencer and Trina, aka Sprina.

BEAUTY AND THE BILLIONAIRE
Edward Quartermaine and Brenda Barrett shared a special relationship; she even went to live with the Quartermaines after one of her many breakups with Sonny.

CLOSE CALL
Mike (center) caused a gas leak at Charlie's Pub, which Sonny (and Julian [Will deVry], right) narrowly escaped. Soon after, Mike admitted he was ready to enter a memory-care facility.

SPOTLIGHT

Close to Home

GH scored again with a real-life story in 2018, diagnosing Sonny's estranged father, Mike (played by Max Gail of *Barney Miller* fame), with Alzheimer's disease and showing his slow deterioration in real time until 2020. "When I started that story, my dad got Alzheimer's, and when I ended the story, Mike died and my dad died," Maurice Benard tells *People*. "It wasn't a story that was difficult for me because was living it."

The show played all the beats between father and son, working through their denial and anger about the disease together. Mike offered a series of apologies to his son for his alcohol and gambling addictions and for abandoning Sonny as a boy, leaving him with an abusive stepfather. Sonny forgave his dad but couldn't bear to be in the room with him at the end, so Mike's late daughter Courtney (played again by Alicia Leigh Willis) appeared as a ghost to take Mike to heaven.

Benard credits Gail and the writing for the success of the three-year arc that swept the Daytime Emmys in 2021, helping the show win for Drama Series, Lead Actor (Benard) and Supporting Actor (Gail)—proving once again that the pain of a loved one facing illness is the most relatable soap tale of all.

'WHEN I STARTED THAT STORY, MY DAD GOT ALZHEIMER'S, AND WHEN I ENDED THE STORY, MIKE DIED AND MY DAD DIED'
—MAURICE BENARD

TROPHY TIME
Gail (below left) and Benard both took home Emmy awards for the story line. Benard closed out his acceptance speech with, "Max Gail, I love you."

NOT SO LUCKY
After years of trauma, Luke and Laura's son Lucky (Jonathan Jackson) left Port Charles in 2011 in search of a simpler life.

JESSIE'S WHIRL
Rick Springfield appeared at the 2013 Nurses' Ball as himself, which must have confused all the characters who interacted with him as Dr. Noah Drake in the past.

FEARLESS LEADER
Under Valentini's leadership, *GH* has won the Daytime Emmy for Best Drama Series five times since 2012.

This magnificent mayhem was presided over by Frank Valentini, who was hired as executive producer in 2012 and had to navigate budget cuts (including accelerating the filming schedule and going dark for weeks at a time) while also expanding the story lines for the show's beloved veteran actors. The global pandemic that began in 2020 presented a historic first, and not a good one: How to stop filming for four months while still putting content on the air every weekday. Valentini recut shows to make the most of scenes that had already been shot, and then ABC aired old episodes until filming could resume.

The actors came back to mandatory vaccination and testing, with COVID advisers on-set to ensure safety protocols were being followed (no smooching!). "We have to give props to Frank Valentini for keeping the show on the air and for bringing it back after the pandemic," praised Maurice Benard (Sonny).

Fortunately, by 2022, kissing had resumed—putting the love back in the afternoon where it belongs.

WHEN NELLE FELL
A fight at the top of the stairs led to a pregnant Nelle (Chloe Lanier) falling down the stairs and Carly being arrested for pushing her scheming rival.

TODAY'S SUPER-COUPLES

Why should young people have all the fun? *GH*'s vets found love, starting with Luke and Laura, who moved on with more realistic partners. Luke indulged his love of adventure by wedding Tracy Quartermaine, who had the money and desire to travel the world with him (which also explained Tony Geary and Jane Elliot's exits from the show in 2017). Laura settled down with Dr. Kevin Collins (Jon Lindstrom) in 2017 and became "Madame Mayor."

Her children haven't been as lucky. Daughter Lulu spent a few quality years with Sonny's son Dante until an explosion meant for Jason at the Floating Rib bar put her in a coma. And son Nikolas Cassadine finally locked down Ava Jerome, but a sex romp with his son Spencer's girlfriend put the kibosh on their happily ever after.

Elizabeth promised "Till death do us part" with Franco Baldwin at their 2019 wedding, which unfortunately became reality two years later when he was murdered by Faison's son Peter. Alexis continued her pattern of choosing unsuitable men (criminal Sonny, killer Jerry Jacks, a very married Ned Quartermaine) by falling for Mob scion Julian Jerome (Will deVry). Julian died in 2020 during a fight with Sonny, which left PC's favorite mobster with amnesia—a convenient excuse when Sonny fell for Nina while married to Carly. Carly's response when Sonny regained his memory? Forget it. They divorced...again.

FRANCO'S REBOOT
When Franco was recast with popular actor Roger Howarth, his life of crime was explained away by a brain tumor that had caused him to act violently.

CHRISTMAS MIRACLE
Laura wed Kevin during an ice storm in December 2017, promising, "I will love you every day for the rest of my life." So far, so good!

SPOOKED BY FLUKE
Lucy officiated at Luke and Tracy's wedding during the 2014 Nurses' Ball. Tracy later had the marriage annulled when it turned out she had actually wed one of Luke's alternate personalities.

THE *PEOPLE* INTERVIEWS

The Cast *Tells* All

THE CURRENT CAST FEATURES BELOVED VETERANS AND INTRIGUING NEWCOMERS. HERE THEY REMINISCE ABOUT FAVORITE STORY LINES AND OPEN UP ABOUT LIFE ON (AND OFF) THE SET.

'OLDER LAURA IS LOOKING TO GIVE LOVE. THAT'S A NICE FLIP, AS IT SHOULD BE. HER MOTHERLY INSTINCTS ARE DIRECTED MORE TOWARD THE TOWN'
—GENIE FRANCIS

THE SON ALSO RISES
"I wanted Laura to have a secret," Francis says, revealing that it was her idea for Laura to have given birth when she was abducted by Stavros Cassadine in the 1980s. That child grew up to be Nikolas Cassadine (Marcus Coloma), a troublemaker who supports his mom—when not battling with his wife, Ava (Maura West, left).

GENIE FRANCIS
as LAURA COLLINS

If Port Charles has a beating heart, it rests with Laura—whose own has been courted too many times to count. "You know what her name is?" Genie Francis asks with a laugh. "Laura Vining Faulkner Webber Baldwin Spencer Cassadine Spencer Collins Webber Collins."

46 Years of Story—and Counting

She won't name her favorite "husband" for fear of hurting her many leading men, but she will name her favorite story line: Those summers on the run. "The two I did with Tony [Geary, aka Luke] were fantastic," the actress says. "I loved the comeback with little Jonathan Jackson [who played her son Lucky], because now we had a triangle to work with. Those were exciting, groundbreaking, fun times."

That first summer was groundbreaking all right, coming on the heels of Laura's controversial rape turned "seduction" in 1979 when both the actress and the character were teenagers. "There are so many things that happened back then that I hope would never happen today," says Francis, adding that Geary sent her flowers the day they filmed those difficult scenes at the Campus Disco. "He was so protective of me. He treated me like I was a little

China doll. Tony Geary was the most gentlemanly with sex and love scenes of anybody I worked with. I got the prince first, then I got the frogs!"

The Emmy winner remembers being "shocked" when Elizabeth Taylor asked if she could attend Luke and Laura's wedding (as Helena Cassadine, who put a curse on the couple). "I didn't understand how big it all was. I was a kid! I had such a tiny little life, from my bedroom to the studio to school and back to my bedroom to learn my lines."

Francis didn't even get to keep the champagne sent to her by the only bride more famous than she was in 1981. "Somebody said, 'This is from the Right Honorable Lady Diana Spencer, and we wanted you to know.' But they didn't give me the champagne because I was underage."

Beyond Port Charles

Francis expanded her "tiny little life" in 1982 by leaving *GH* to take on numerous other daytime and primetime roles, including the miniseries *North and South*, where she started dating Jonathan Frakes (who gained fame as Will Riker on *Star Trek: The Next Generation*). They wed in 1988 and made a point of taking summers off so they could give their two children a far more normal childhood than Francis had. "I wanted a period of time where we stopped and were just a family, because both my husband and I worked on franchise shows," she explains.

Embracing the Craziness

Francis has come to terms with the crazy fame of the Luke and Laura franchise, saying it has settled down to where she feels that now "everywhere I go I have friends." The same could be said of Laura, who has come full circle by getting elected mayor of Port Charles, the city she took by storm back in 1977. "Her motherly instincts are directed more toward the town now," says the actress. "Young Laura was desperately looking for love and to be loved. Older Laura is looking to give love—as it should be."

'I WATCHED THIS SHOW AS A CHILD AND LOVED IT. I WANTED TO BE THE BLACK LUKE SPENCER!'
—DONNELL TURNER

Donnell Turner *as* CURTIS ASHFORD

Hired in 2015, Donnell Turner came on as "a former drug addict who broke into places and was married to his brother's widow, Jordan," the actor recalls. He quickly flipped the script—literally. "They told me, 'Tell our story, but use your verbiage,' so there was a lot of line changing."

If you heard Curtis's initial exchange with Hayden (Rebecca Budig), you know what he's talking about. "My third episode, Curtis was waiting outside Kelly's. Hayden walks up, and the line was 'Where've you been? I'm out here freezing.' I said 'I'm out here freezing my Black ass off.' It aired. Frank [Valentini, executive producer] loved it. Daytime isn't what it used to be. I thought, 'Let me take some culture to our competition.' I don't want to change what's been working for 60 years, I just want to offer something different."

Curtis became a private investigator, and Turner opened a dialogue with the writers about other ways his character—and the show—could evolve. "There was no Black home ownership, no Black nuclear family, no Black father figures on the show," Turner says. "I see the mansions of the Quartermaines and the Corinthoses, and none of them belong to Black people. These are things I addressed."

Fast-forward to 2023, and Curtis is getting married to Dr. Portia Robinson, helping raise her daughter Trina, and living in Jax's former beach house, which they purchased. "I love the writers for hearing me when I spoke about this," Turner says. "We have a responsibility and a privilege to show the aspirational side of life, as well."

And as a lifelong fan of the show, he admits it's been a surreal experience to work alongside actors like Genie Francis and Anthony Geary. "Every day," responds Turner, "my 10-year-old self is high-fiving me!"

MAURICE BENARD

as SONNY CORINTHOS

Maurice Benard remembers clearly the advice he was given on his first day at *General Hospital* in 1993. He didn't take it. "The director Joe Behar said 'Talk louder,'" Benard says, "and I remember making the decision not to. I needed to act in a way that was comfortable for me. Thirty years later here we are."

Indeed, the California native has shepherded Sonny from struggling strip club owner to successful "coffee importer" (read: mobster) by following his

'THE BEST ANSWER I CAN GIVE IS LOVE THE ONE YOU'RE WITH!'
—MAURICE BENARD, ON WHO MIGHT BE SONNY'S TRUE LOVE

instincts. "I don't like to run lines," he says. "When I get to the set, I've already prepared. Let's make it spontaneous."

He keeps his three Daytime Emmys for Outstanding Lead Actor "in a glass thing in my house" as reward for that spontaneity but confesses he wasn't sold on the story that led up to his most recent award. "I told Cynthia [Watros, who plays Nina] the first day, 'This is probably not going to work. Let's just have fun.'" His reluctance had more to do with Sonny's temporary amnesia ("I was Cowboy Mike") than with his character's new love interest Nina. "Cynthia is incredibly talented. All I care about is the person in front of me. Is she talented? Can she act? That makes me happy."

The Pursuit of Happiness

Offscreen, that contentment has proven elusive for the actor, who has been open about his struggles. He's worked tirelessly with the National Mental Health Association (NMHA) on the importance of recognizing the signs and symptoms of bipolar disorder—a condition that also afflicts his character—and records a popular podcast, *State of Mind With Maurice Benard*, which has more than 100,000 subscribers.

Benard has spent more than 30 years with his wife, Paula, but admits even she couldn't help him when the pandemic hit and *GH* stopped taping for four months. "The shutdown threw me for a loop," he says. "It wasn't bipolar, it was anxiety. It felt like the end of the world in my mind." He eventually sorted it out and hopes the dark days are behind him. "I go to the grocery store and talk to everybody now," says the father of four. "It's like how normal people must feel."

Finding His Groove

Stepping back into Sonny's shoes helped, as did playing a lighter story line in which he "truly" believes his character loves Nina. Which is not to say Benard wouldn't welcome a reunion with Sonny's most significant other loves, Carly and Brenda. "It would be great if Brenda came back. They were a great match."

Kristina Wagner *as* FELICIA JONES SCORPIO

Feelings spilled over for the young actress and Jack Wagner, who played Felicia's lover Frisco Jones, in 1984. They married, had two children and later divorced. Wagner's role at *GH* has grown since Frisco exited in 1995. Felicia found happiness with Mac Scorpio, opened a thriving PI business and has become a doting grandma. But the former Aztec princess hasn't lost her edge: She killed long-running villain Peter August with a tire iron last year after he threatened her daughter Maxie.

Sadly, her son Harrison died in 2022 at age 27 from an accidental overdose of fentanyl and alprazolam. "I don't know how we survive grief," tweeted Kristina, responding to donations made in Harrison Wagner's name to New Life House, a sober living community for young men. "Perhaps through the kindness of people."

Josh Swickard *as* HARRISON CHASE

Swickard's former police officer, who goes by Chase, fell for Willow Tait when he came to Port Charles in 2018. He moved on to Brook Lynn Quartermaine when they worked together on his singing career, making beautiful music until Chase learned Brook Lynn had sabotaged his efforts to get back on the PC police force. Swickard, a former model, has scored better in real life—he and his wife, Lauren, expect their second child in 2023.

Leslie Charleson *as* DR. MONICA QUARTERMAINE

Missouri native Leslie Charleson checked into the hospital in 1977 and quickly moved front burner playing a skilled cardiologist who couldn't operate matters of the heart. A messy love triangle with brothers Jeff and Rick Webber evolved into a messier one with Rick and Lesley until Monica met wealthy Dr. Alan Quartermaine, and sparks flew for the next three decades.

The hiring of Stuart Damon as Alan in 1977 resulted in a lifelong friendship for Charleson. "I'd drive up in my '72 Cougar convertible," she says of giving Damon (who passed away in 2021) a ride to work each day after he joined the show. "Stuart would joke, 'Having a blonde pick me up in a convertible in Hollywood—it doesn't get any better than this!'" Their warm feelings didn't extend to their on-set battles, though. "We'd do real slaps," Charleson reveals. "Stuart was always afraid I'd take his eye out. I would fake a slap in dress rehearsal, but when we went to tape it, all that went out the window!"

Charleson remains *GH*'s longest-running current player (despite some recent health issues) and the valuable matriarch of the Quartermaine clan.

NICHOLAS CHAVEZ *as* SPENCER CASSADINE & TABYANA ALI *as* TRINA ROBINSON

Spencer and Trina weren't even an official couple when fans assigned them a "squish" name: Sprina. "I'm taken aback by all the good feedback and positive comments," Tabyana Ali says, theorizing that it's "the angst" causing people to respond so favorably. "We are showing the audience what it's like to long for somebody."

"It's fun to go online," adds Nicholas Chavez, who plays Spencer. "It's like rave reviews every time." He says landing the role of Laura's black sheep grandson in 2021—his first professional acting job "was probably the coolest moment of my life so far." Less than a year later he won the Daytime Emmy for Outstanding Younger Performer in a Drama Series. "Twelve months before I received that award, I was selling cars in Florida, so it was a paradigm shift of epic proportions," he told *People* in 2022. "It was very, very surreal to stand up on that stage and be recognized for the thing that I'm more passionate about than anything else."

Worth the Wait

Credit the couple's popularity to *GH*'s trademark skill at scripting star-crossed teens. Trina almost went to jail after being framed by Spencer's ex-girlfriend Esme, and Spencer's been to jail twice (so far) for crimes also instigated by Esme. The denial of their feelings for each other combined with, as Ali says, "the longing," secured Sprina's place as one of the hottest young couples in soaps. That, and the actors' chemistry. "Nick is a passionate person when it comes to his work," says Ali. "That's why we do such good work, because of how dedicated he is."

Not that Ali isn't holding her own. She found her stride quickly after replacing Sydney Mikayla in the role in early 2022 after Mikayla quit to attend college. "Nick gave me pointers on what he and Sydney used to do and caught me up on the story line. He made sure I was okay when I first started. We've been good friends to each other."

Which translates to the screen in their scenes together. "When you miss somebody, it makes you love them even more," says Ali. "It's Sprina nation, you know?"

'TRINA AND SPENCER SEE EACH OTHER, AND IT'S PASSION AND FIRE'
—**TABYANA ALI**

Kin Shriner *as* SCOTTY BALDWIN

Scotty began his Port Charles life in 1977 as an eager law student madly in love with an innocent teenager named Laura (perhaps you've heard of her). "There were no supercouples back then, so it was all new," Shriner recalled to *Soap Opera Digest* in 2012. "After about a year, Genie and I took a trip to Fort Lauderdale, and we were having dinner at a place called Stan's on the water. Somewhere after our conch chowder we looked up, and there were people asking for our autograph. The line snaked all the way downstairs and out the block. I said to Genie, 'We might be onto something!'"

Tune in nearly half a century later, and you'll find ace attorney Scotty still bringing the drama in the courtroom—and still sharing scenes with Laura.

Katelyn MacMullen *as* WILLOW TAIT

A former child model for Disney and Mattel, MacMullen has been busy since joining GH in 2018. Her character was raised in a cult and became pregnafnt by its evil leader Shiloh. She gave the baby up for adoption to protect it, then it died, and then it was switched with the boy Nelle had given birth to (fathered by Michael Corinthos). Fast forward to 2023 and Willow is a nurse living happily ever after with Michael and little Wiley. Well, except for her leukemia.

REBECCA HERBST *as* ELIZABETH WEBBER

Rebecca Herbst has a problem: She has had chemistry with every leading man *GH* has paired her with for the last 25 years. That makes it hard for viewers to move on when her character does, sparking many furious debates online.

"Those groups are die-hard fans, and I could not love them more," Herbst says. "They are the reason certain couples have stayed relevant and survived. I appreciate their passion, truly!"

As fans argue Lucky vs. Jason vs. Franco, let's go to the source for Nurse Webber's true love. "If you look at Elizabeth's life as a whole, it's a toss-up between Lucky and Jason," the actress says. "Lucky was her true love for a big portion of her young life. Jason was her true love as she was becoming an adult. It's hard to compare those two." Liz also enjoyed a few good years with Franco before he died. "Franco came in when she was already a mom and had a career," she says. "Each relationship served a different purpose in her life."

Like her character, Herbst has three children (with husband Michael Saucedo, who played Juan on *GH*) and one of them has even appeared on the show—sort of. "When they showed Elizabeth's ultrasound of her third child, Aiden, they used my real video from my little Emerson," she reveals. "That was really special."

Feeling Lucky

Asked for her favorite story, it's Lucky Spencer all the way. "I have such fond memories of the original Liz and Lucky days working with Jonathan Jackson," she says. "They were two innocent children who came from complicated backgrounds trying to navigate the world together. Camping out in the boxcar and getting into trouble together was a lot of fun."

Three different actors have played Luke and Laura's son, proving that the actress earned her A+ on all those chemistry tests. "I was lucky to end up with some really great Luckys," she says with a laugh. "Jacob Young's time was short-lived. I have more memories of working with Greg Vaughn; I absolutely adore him. He embodied a more mature Lucky. It would be amazing if he came back."

Hey, it could happen. *GH* brought Jeff Webber and his wife, Carolyn, back in 2022. "I'm super glad that after 25 years I got to have parents," quips Herbst. "That was nice."

++

'WHEN I FIRST JOINED, I THOUGHT, "THIS IS A COOL ACTING GIG THAT WILL LAST A FEW YEARS." IT'S BECOME A WAY OF LIFE, MY SECOND FAMILY, MY HOME AWAY FROM HOME'

—REBECCA HERBST

FINOLA HUGHES

as ANNA DEVANE

"Gloria Monty brought me to her office and said she wanted me to watch a Joan Crawford movie called *A Woman's Face,*" Finola Hughes says of her introduction to the show in 1985. "She said, 'That's what we're going to do to you.'"

"That" was a facial scar to be sported by Hughes's character, a permanent Scarlet Letter resulting from a mysterious betrayal in her past.

But when the fans took to Anna, the writers ditched the scar and gave her a dramatic story with ex-husband Robert (Tristan Rogers) and Robert's shady wife, Holly (Emma Samms). That love triangle was revisited when Samms returned to *GH* in 2022. "We all came up through the ranks with the same executive producer Gloria Monty, so it was really lovely," Hughes says of the reunion.

Maternal Instincts

The other story that put Anna on the Port Charles map was the "Asian Quarter" story back in the '80s with her daughter Robin (Kimberly McCullough). "We went to Chinatown in Vancouver and shot in back alleys with these amazing Asian actors," Hughes recalls. "We were shooting on the street with a photograph of Robin: 'Have you seen this child?' It was very real. When I found her, we pulled the van in and did it in one take. Kimberly was an extraordinary little actor."

The mom of three is grateful that Anna has had "pretty great pairings" with Robert, Duke, Finn and now Valentin Cassadine (James Patrick Stuart). "We're on this Vanna train, and people are really responding to this partnership. Sometimes when we do a scene, James will say, 'Oh they're really going to like this!'"

++

'OUR JOB IS TO BRING EMOTIONAL STORIES INTO THE HOME EVERY DAY, AND *GH* IS FULL OF ACTORS WHO BRING THEIR A GAME AND WORK SO HARD'

—FINOLA HUGHES

Actually, it's been 38 years of fans really liking Anna, on *GH* and on *All My Children* (where she crossed over from 1999-2003). "Having a passion for this medium has fueled me. We have a great leader in Frank [Valentini], and I love our audience—people who are badass and get it."

None more than Hughes herself, who parlayed a short-term Scarface into a four-decade Superspy. "They decided she was an important character, so I stayed and stayed and stayed!"

Chad Duell *as* MICHAEL CORINTHOS III

The Arizona native took over the role of Carly and A.J. Quartermaine's son in 2010. Michael was later adopted by Sonny when he was married to Carly, making Michael the scion of two of PC's biggest families. Duell won a Daytime Emmy in 2015, the year Michael found out his biological dad, A.J., was murdered by his stepfather, Sonny—proving the more drama the better when it comes to awards.

Amanda Setton *as* BROOK LYNN QUARTERMAINE

Setton played Penelope on *Gossip Girl* before joining *GH* as the daughter of Ned and Lois. Named for the birthplace of her mother, Brook Lynn is a troublemaking spitfire in the image of her grandmother Tracy Quartermaine. She faked a pregnancy with Valentin Cassadine to get his shares of her family stock (ELQ International) and schemed to keep her boyfriend Chase off the Port Charles Police Department so he would sing for her burgeoning music company. Tracy would be proud.

NANCY LEE GRAHN *as* ALEXIS DAVIS

Twenty-seven years in, the portrayer of PC's favorite alcoholic ex-attorney says she's finished with the whole sex-symbol thing. "I've done many a love montage, but at a certain point the director says, 'What can I show?' I say 'Nothing!' "

That wasn't the case a few years back when *GH* paired Alexis with Mob scion Julian Jerome (Will deVry) and sparks flew all the way to her bedroom. "The sex was fun," Grahn says. "The knife not so much. But that's just me—a lot of people liked it."

Sure, Julian pulled a dagger on Alexis (which she ended up stabbing him with), but since when is that a deal breaker on soaps? Their romance wasn't really over until Julian died in 2020. Since then, Alexis has focused on her sobriety and her three daughters, Sam, Molly and Kristina, the latter of whom she shares with local mobster Sonny Corinthos. "My dream story is for Alexis to become the Godmother to a rival Mob and take over the Port Charles territory," Grahn says. And then? "Sonny breaks barware." Regardless of what's ahead for Alexis, the Emmy-winning actress says she's prepared for it. "Time is money, and money keeps getting cut, as do rehearsals," Grahn says of the current work schedule at *GH*. "Rehearsals are now only for prime-time actors—or wimps, as we refer to them."

Kelly Monaco & Dominic Zamprogna *as* SAM MCCALL AND DANTE FALCONERI

They're the "soapiest" couple on daytime TV . Sam was married to Jason Morgan (who died twice) while Dante's ex-wife Lulu Spencer is currently in a coma. Sam's mother, Alexis, slept with Dante's father, Sonny, and had a child, so Sam's half sister Kristina is also Dante's half sister. Got that? Sam also slept with Sonny and became pregnant, but she lost the baby; otherwise Dante would be living with his half sibling's mother. And don't forget the time mobster Sonny shot good cop Dante in the chest before he knew Dante was his son.

Real life has been much kinder to this duo. Monaco, who was a *Playboy* Playmate of the Month in April 1997, gained prime-time fame—and a mirror ball trophy—by winning the first season of *Dancing With the Stars* with partner Alec Mazo. Zamprogna, a former child actor in Canada, where his parents ran a dance school, is raising three daughters in L.A. with his wife, Linda Leslie.

James Patrick Stewart *as* VALENTIN CASSADINE

Stuart, whose father, Chad Stuart, was one-half of the famed 1960s British musical duo Chad & Jeremy ("A Summer Song"), is recognizable to pop culture fans as the bellhop in *Pretty Woman* and the furniture maker who sang "Desperado" to Elaine on *Seinfeld*. When not wooing Anna Devane on *GH,* the actor has a thriving career doing voice-over work, records his own music and stars on the Disney Channel sitcom *The Villains of Valley View*.

Brook Kerr *as* DR. PORTIA ROBINSON

The Indianapolis native gave birth to her son Chris Warren Jr. (who grew up to star in *High School Musical*) at age 16 and went on to appear in music videos with Kenny Chesney and Michael Jackson before spending eight years as Whitney Russell on the supernatural soap *Passions*. Her *GH* character has been living with a secret for 20 years: Daughter Trina is suspected of being fathered by Curtis, not Portia's ex-husband Taggert, giving new meaning to the phrase "Physician, heal thyself."

Maura West *as* AVA JEROME

When she looks back on her 2013 entrance, one thing stands out for Maura West: Working with Anthony Geary and Jane Elliot. "That's one of the highlights of my entire career," West says. "A highlight of my life, really. Ava was pretending [her daughter] Kiki was Franco's daughter and living at the Quartermaine mansion. It was delicious, soapy stuff to play."

West knew a little something about delicious, soapy stuff before joining *GH* because she had starred on *As the World Turns* for 15 years (as Carly Tenney Snyder). Luckily she was well acquainted with former *ATWT* costar Jon Lindstrom before he took her hostage on *GH*. "My favorite story was Ava falling in love with someone who she thought was Kevin but turned out to be crazy Ryan Chamberlain, and part of that is because I love Jon Lindstrom," says West. "My other favorite was the Ava and Morgan love affair—and, of course, getting to work with the queen Genie Francis. There's that!"

The three-time Emmy winner is looking forward to what's ahead for her character. "One of the things I love about Ava is that she can be a part of any story, and I would believe it. She's super feminine on one hand, but she can flip and get down and dirty."

Lynn Herring *as* LUCY COE

Her 1986 gig as a timid librarian in love with a killer was supposed to be short term, but producers quickly realized fans loved Lucy and began linking her with a succession of men, including Jake, Tony, Alan, Scotty and Kevin. "Scotty was Lucy's equal in high jinks and farce," says Lynn Herring, who also starred in the show's 1997-2003 spinoff *Port Charles*. "But Kevin was her passion." It remains to be seen whether new flame Martin Grey will light Lucy's fire or fizzle out.

Herring's favorite role remains hosting the annual Nurses' Ball to raise AIDS awareness. The black tie songfest features a running gag that leaves Lucy exposed in her underwear that began as the result of a wardrobe change gone awry. "The audience gets to laugh and cry," says Herring. "That's when television is at its best—when it's creating art with a purpose."

Tristan Rogers *as* ROBERT SCORPIO

After creating the role of the Aussie secret agent Robert Scorpio in 1980, Tristan Rogers was derailed by a "fatal" boat explosion in 1992, only to reappear, dapper as ever, in 2006. He's currently keeping Port Charles safe as district attorney and remains a lively fixture in ex-wife Anna Devane's life. "I've seen this show at its best and at something less than that," says the actor. Scorpio's 2022 romantic reunion with Holly Sutton (the returning Emma Samms) was surely *GH* at its best. All the times Scorpio "died" or lapsed into a coma? Something less than that.

KIRSTEN STORMS *as* MAXIE JONES

Maxie has survived a heart transplant, a murder rap and the loss of her husband (Nathan) and sister (Georgie), proving she's a force of nature akin to her supercouple parents, Frisco and Felicia. The same could be said of Kirsten Storms, whose life has veered toward soap opera as well, starting with her public battle with endometriosis while married to Brandon Barash (who played *GH* mobster Johnny Zacchara). "It was pretty bleak as far as the probability of her being able to get pregnant," Barash told *People* in 2013, "but then we got back from a trip to Amsterdam and discovered we were expecting. We calculated that we conceived the baby in [former *GH* star] Tony Geary's guest room!"

Daughter Harper was born in 2014; Storms and Barash split in 2016. In 2021 a headache-plagued Storms underwent brain surgery and had to sport wigs during her recovery. "I'm immensely thankful to my 'work family,' who have been supportive, kind and loving," she wrote on Instagram. "They shaved a portion of my head, so please no comments if you don't like my hair. It's temporary."

CYNTHIA WATROS
as NINA REEVES

Cynthia Watros had her work cut out for her when she took over the role of Nina Reeves from the popular Michelle Stafford in 2019—and then even more so when *GH* paired Nina with Sonny. "I know it was challenging for fans," Watros acknowledges of the 2021 story line where Sonny was presumed dead, turned up in Nixon Falls with amnesia and fell for Nina. The challenge, of course, was that Sonny was married to Carly at the time, and Nina kept her mouth shut.

Sonny and Nina are back in Port Charles now, where she is universally hated by his family (especially Carly). Nina doesn't care. "What Nina is experiencing with Sonny is this slow love affair that she's never had," Watros says. "They are both accepting each other for who they are; it's a different kind of love. If you think about your high school boyfriend, it was so intense! It feels different when you fall in love in your 40s."

Fans know that Willow, who has a child with Sonny and Carly's son Michael, is the daughter Nina searched for and believed was dead. "Everyone knew that but Nina," says Watros, who won a Daytime Emmy in 1998 for playing Annie Dutton on *Guiding Light* and starred on the prime-time hit *Lost*. "She has a big hole in her heart about her daughter that was taken from her." For those doing the math at home, that means Carly and Nina share a grandchild, which will give Nina ammunition to battle her rival for years to come.

Jon Lindstrom
as RYAN CHAMBERLAIN & DR. KEVIN COLLINS

As soap hoppers go, Jon Lindstrom might hold the record. He was on *Santa Barbara* before joining *GH* as serial killer Ryan, took on the role of Ryan's twin, Kevin, two years later, crossed Kevin over to *Port Charles*, then hopped to *As The World Turns* (where he fell for now wife Cady McClain, who had previously played Dixie on *All My Children*) before bringing Kevin and Ryan back to *GH*. Whew! In between counseling at *GH* and dealing with his nutty brother and his brother's nutty daughter Esme, Kevin is by the side of the queen of Port Charles: his wife, Laura.

John J. York *as* MAC SCORPIO

Mac holds a singular place in *GH* history having only been married to one woman (Felicia) in 32 years on the show and having only worked at one professional job (for the PCPD). He also gets props for raising his niece Robin and stepdaughters Maxie and Georgie. Felicia likes to call him "Grumpy Grampa" when they're babysitting Maxie's kids, but he's the sweetest—and least complicated!—grandfather around.

While Mac enjoys one of *GH*'s longest unions with Felicia, York's real-life marriage to Vicki has lasted even longer. "I was waiting tables at the Cheesecake Factory, and my wife was seven and a half months pregnant," he recalls of his life when he auditioned for *GH*. "Jan. 14 [1991] was my first day, and three weeks later, on Feb. 9, my daughter Schyler was born." (Schyler now has kids of her own!) "This job was the greatest gift to me, because I was home for dinner, made her breakfast, got to walk her to school every day," York says. "I'm very blessed." A favorite memory? "When Schyler started talking, I would say, 'Where does Daddy work?' She'd say 'Genital Hospital!' I guess that's true in a lot of ways."

Eden McCoy *as* JOSSLYN JACKS

Born in 2009 to Carly and Jax, Josslyn was rapidly aged in 2015 to partake in the PC teen scene. She lost her virginity to Liz's son Cameron in 2022, an act which was deviously recorded by Esmé and released to the world. Fortunately the only public drama Josslyn's portrayer has faced is whether to bump or spike the ball on the beach volleyball team she plays on while attending USC. Scoring means something entirely different when you're on a soap!

LAURA WRIGHT
AS CARLY SPENCER

She's the fourth actress to play Carly, but after 17 years Laura Wright has made the role her own. And nothing pleased her more than when *GH* changed her character's last name to Spencer in 2022, reflecting Carly's heritage as the daughter of famed hooker turned nurse Bobbie Spencer and niece of some guy named Luke. "When I started, I was Carly Alcazar," Wright recalls. "Then Carly Corinthos, Carly Jacks, then for 24 hours Carly Morgan. I grew up watching *General Hospital,* so to think that I'm a Spencer now blows my mind. I love it!"

Wright's not kidding when she says she grew up watching the soap. "My favorite story of all time was when Laura returned and Luke saw her on the balcony [in 1983]. She was wearing a cloak, and he dropped the glass of brandy and ran to her. I remember screaming on my bed with delight! I think I was 12."

In terms of story lines, the actress can't narrow it down to just one of her personal favorites, but she puts Jax and Carly's romance, the dynamic of Carly, Sonny and Jason, and all the times Carly has gone out on a limb for her kids all at the top of her list. "The most challenging scenes I've had were when Michael was shot and when Morgan died," Wright says. "When you bury a child, that changes you forever." Michael's shooting changed him forever too. "He went into a coma as a cute little redhead and woke up as a 16-year-old with a six-pack. Only in daytime!"

Fans would probably point to Carly's ex-husbands (and fathers of her kids) Sonny and Jax as the loves of her life, but Wright begs to differ. "It's Jason of course! He was always her best friend who accepted her for who she was. Your true love doesn't have to be the person you lay your head down with every night."

Jason died in 2021, so it's onward for the never-say-die and newly named Ms. Spencer. "Carly is one of the best roles on daytime television," says Wright. "Strong, vulnerable, flawed and so authentically her. I'm so grateful I get to play her."

Wally Kurth *as* NED QUARTERMAINE

Having tough Tracy Quartermaine for a mother prepared young Ned for a lifetime of infighting over his family's company ELQ, but it was still a surprise when he donned a pair of leather pants in the mid-1990s to assume a double life as a rock star. "It was fun to incorporate my passion for singing when my real-life band portrayed my fictional band Eddie Maine and the Idle Rich," recalls Wally Kurth, citing Ned's foray into the music world as his favorite story.

"Eddie" started wooing a gorgeous record producer named Lois, which was a problem, because Ned was already being forced into marriage by Katherine Bell. "It had everything you need in a classic Quartermaine story: blackmail, backpedaling and bigamy! The writers and producers also created a truly romantic and entertaining love story between Ned and Lois."

Life imitated art when Kurth fell in love with Rena Sofer, who played Lois. They married and had a daughter, as did Ned and Lois (Brook Lynn, now grown and a businesswoman). Both couples split: Kurth is now wed to Debra while Ned found happiness with Sonny's ex Olivia Falconeri. And after 32 years on the show, Kurth says he's still "living the dream," despite Ned having ditched those leather pants long ago.

BEHIND THE SCENES

Home Base

EXEC PRODUCER FRANK VALENTINI AND STAR **LAURA WRIGHT** OFFER A GUIDED TOUR OF CARLY'S BELOVED KITCHEN

BRIGHT IDEA
School schedules and artwork (updated as Carly and Sonny's kids get older) add authenticity to the kitchen, but executive producer Frank Valentini says they also have a practical purpose. "[They] help block the reflection from the fridge in the cameras."

THINK SINK
"The soap and dishwashing stuff is clear, so you can have it without it being [tied to] a brand," says Valentini. Carly, he adds, has a window over her sink so she can "rinse her coffee mug and daydream about Drew and what life would have been like if Jason had lived."

SHELF LIFE
"The copper mugs were expensive," offers Valentini. "They match the cocktail shakers, and the gold bricks match the chandelier. [Production designer] Jennifer [Elliott] was very specific about the mugs being big and heavy… to feel like a proper cup of coffee in contrast to the teacups in the Quartermaine mansion."

MOSS IS BOSS
Valentini had no idea that when production designer Elliott placed an innocuous bowl of moss on the new set of the Corinthos kitchen in 2019 it would soon trend on Twitter. "I think what caught [viewers'] attention is that it's unusual," Valentini says. "The idea that the same moss that grows on a rock is in the middle of someone's kitchen is funny." Adds Laura Wright, who plays Carly: "We took the moss out for summer and got complaints: 'Where's the moss?' Now it's a thing. When we brought it back, we posted it on Instagram!"

DRY WINE
Of Carly's well-stocked wine cabinet, "The bottles are real, but it's nonalcoholic wine and sparkling water," Valentini says. "We have a 'no alcohol' building."

'IT'S FUNNY WHAT PEOPLE GET HOOKED ON'
—LAURA WRIGHT

GUEST STARS

Visiting Hours

CELEBRITY FANS HAVE OFTEN CHECKED IN FOR BRIEF STAYS IN THE *HOSPITAL*

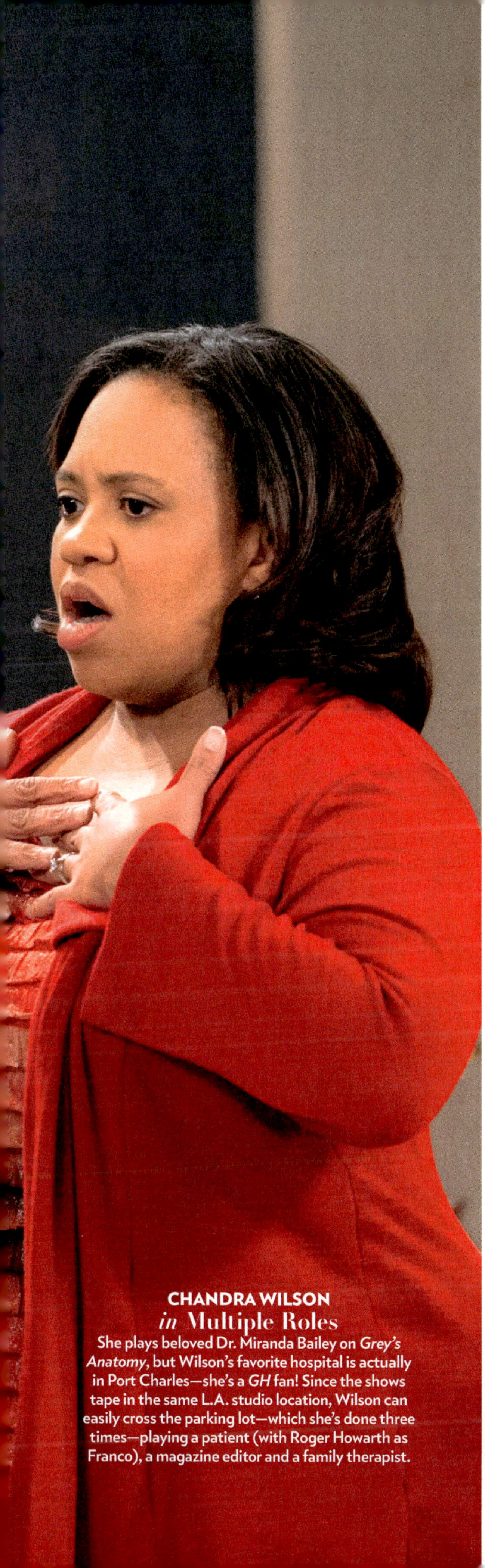

ELIZABETH TAYLOR *as* **Helena Cassadine**

The guest star to top all guest stars appeared for five episodes during the Luke and Laura extravaganza—and placed a curse on the newlyweds. "Luke and Laura's love story made Elizabeth feel very nostalgic," Anthony Geary recalled to *TV Guide Magazine* in 2014. "She said it reminded her of her youth and the great romance films of the old studio system."

JAMES FRANCO *as* **Franco Baldwin**

In 2009 the actor asked *GH* to create a role for him. "Franco" became a Keith Haring-type artist and depraved serial killer fixated on hurting everyone that Jason (Steve Burton) loved. The *127 Hours* star appeared sporadically through 2012. "I wanted to be an artist, and I wanted my character to be crazy," he told *The New Yorker.* Mission accomplished.

CHANDRA WILSON *in* **Multiple Roles**

She plays beloved Dr. Miranda Bailey on *Grey's Anatomy*, but Wilson's favorite hospital is actually in Port Charles—she's a *GH* fan! Since the shows tape in the same L.A. studio location, Wilson can easily cross the parking lot—which she's done three times—playing a patient (with Roger Howarth as Franco), a magazine editor and a family therapist.

YOGI BERRA *as* **Dr. Lawrence Berra**
The Baseball Hall of Famer and 10-time World Series champion (right, with John Beradino as Steve) took a swing at acting, playing a brain surgeon in 1963. "Those were the days before the soaps got sexy," he joked in his book *When You Come to the Fork in the Road, Take It!*

SAMMY DAVIS JR.
as **Eddie Phillips**
By the time Davis appeared on *GH* for a week in 1982—playing a terminally ill dad trying to make peace with his son Bryan (Todd Davis, above left, with Bianca Ferguson as Claudia and Davis)—he was a soaps vet: Earlier the song-and-dance man had appeared on *One Life to Live* and *Love of Life.*

MILTON BERLE
as **Mickey Miller**
Shortly after Elizabeth Taylor's appearance, the veteran comic came to *GH* as an agent who persuades Laura (Genie Francis, left, with Sharon Wyatt as Tiffany) to try modeling.

RICHARD SIMMONS

as Himself

In the late '70s and early '80s, before anyone had heard of *Sweatin' to the Oldies,* the exercise fanatic (left, with Denise Alexander as Lesley Webber) was a frequent visitor, leading classes in the disco. "Gloria Monty was stricter than any Catholic nun who taught me in school," Simmons said of the former exec producer. *GH* exposure helped make his 1980 book *Never-Say-Diet* a huge hit.

MAKSIM CHMERKOVSKIY

as Anton Ivanov

The longtime *Dancing With the Stars* pro (left, with Lynn Herring) waltzed into town in 2013, playing a Metro Court hotel employee who ends up helping choreograph the Nurses' Ball.

SPOTLIGHT

The Alums

BEFORE THEY WERE STARS, THESE FAMOUS FOLK SPENT TIME IN PORT CHARLES

MARK HAMILL

as Kent Murray

A long time ago—1972 to '73, to be precise—and in what must seem like a galaxy far, far away, the *Star Wars* hero played the troubled nephew of Nurse Jessie Brewer.

DEMI MOORE

as Jackie Templeton

The future box office queen played a reporter looking for her missing sister Laura (Janine Turner, later of *Northern Exposure* fame), romanced Robert Scorpio and departed in 1983 to film *Blame It on Rio*. Her next movie, *St. Elmo's Fire*, made her a star.

'I WAS FULLY FAKING IT TILL I MADE IT. I HAD NO CLUE WHAT I WAS DOING'

—DEMI MOORE, ON HER TIME ON *GH*, TO *INTERVIEW* IN 2021

RICKY MARTIN
as **Miguel Morez**
A few years before he was livin' la vida loca, the Puerto Rican pop star spent two years as a hospital orderly-bartender who ultimately left Port Charles to pursue a music career.

JOHN STAMOS
as **Blackie Parrish**
"If I'm anywhere, it's because of *General Hospital*," the *Full House* star said of his two-year gig as a street kid turned musician. "I'll never stop appreciating what *GH* meant to me.

Meghan's Debut

Before her breakout gig on *Suits*—and her role of a lifetime as the Duchess of Sussex and wife of Prince Harry (above)—Meghan Markle landed her first TV part on *GH* in 2002. (Her father, Thomas Markle, was a longtime lighting director on the show.) Appearing in one episode as a nurse named Jill, she had barely any dialogue, but it got her acting resumé started.

JONATHAN JACKSON & AMBER TAMBLYN
as **Lucky Spencer & Emily Quartermaine**
As the golden child of Luke and Laura, Jackson won five Daytime Emmys during his time on *GH*. He parlayed that role to a splashy gig on *Nashville*. Tamblyn, who played the long-suffering adopted daughter of Alan and Monica, also went on to prime-time success (*Joan of Arcadia*) as well as the film, *Sisterhood of the Traveling* Pants.

Credits

FRONT COVER
(Devane), (Webber, Spencer) Ricky Middlesworth/ABC

1 Nick Argo/ABC/Getty Images; **5** Troy Harvey/ABC/ Getty Images; **6-7** ABC-TV/ Kobal/Shutterstock; **13** (top) ABC Photo Archives/Getty Images; **27** (Monty) ABC Photo Archives/Disney General Entertainment Content/Getty Images; **38-40** ABC Photo Archives/Disney General Entertainment Content/Getty Images; **50** (Kurth/Sofer), **51** Jonathan Exley/Contour by Getty Images(2); **52-53** Jeffrey Mayer/ Disney General Entertainment Content/Getty Images; **58** (Sam/Jason) Greg Zabilski/ Disney General Entertainment Content/Getty Images; **62** Rick Rowell/Disney General Entertainment Content/Getty Images; **63** XJJohnson/JPI; **64** (Jackson) Alberto E. Rodriguez/Getty Images; (Valentini) Earl Gibson III/ Getty Images; **65** XJJohnson/ JPI; **67** (from top) Todd Wawrychuk/ABC/Getty Images; Rick Rowell/Disney General Entertainment Content/Getty Images; **68-69** Ricky Middlesworth/ ABC; **70** Christopher Willard/ ABC/Getty Images; **71** Craig Sjodin/ABC; **72** Todd Wawrychuk/ABC; **73** (from top) Ricky Middlesworth/ABC; Craig Sjodin/ABC; **74** Craig Sjodin/ABC; **75** Ali Ricky Middlesworth/ABC; **76-77** (from left) Craig Sjodin/ ABC; Ricky Middlesworth/ ABC; **78** Ricky Middlesworth/ ABC; **79** (from top) Todd Wawrychuk/ABC; Ricky Middlesworth/ABC; **80** (clockwise from top left) Image Group LA/ABC/Getty Images; Ricky Middlesworth/ ABC; Craig Sjodin/ABC; **81** (from left) Ricky Middlesworth/ABC; Todd Wawrychuk/ABC; **82** (clockwise from top left) ABC; Todd Wawrychuk/ABC; Nick Argo/ABC; **84** Ricky Middlesworth/ABC(4); **85** (from left) Todd Wawrychuk/ABC; Ricky Middlesworth/ABC; **86-87** (from left) Ricky Middlesworth/ABC; ABC; **88** Todd Wawrychuk/ABC/ Getty Images' **89** (Burton/ Franco) Chris Chavira/Disney General Entertainment Content/Getty Images; **90** (Berra) Sporting News/ Getty Images; **91** (Chmerkovskiy) Howard Wise/JPI; **92** (Hamill) ABC Photo Archives/Getty Images; (Moore) Erik Hein/ABC/ Getty Images; **93** (clockwise from bottom left) ABC Photo Archives/Disney General Entertainment Content/ Getty Images; Craig Sjodin/ Disney General Entertainment Content/Getty Images; Patrick van Katwijk/Getty Images; ABC; **94** Craig Sjodin/ABC/ Getty Images; **96** (Geary/ Shriner) ABC Photo Archives/ Disney General Entertainment Content/Getty Images

BACK COVER
(top, from left) Rick Rowell/ Disney General Entertainment Content/Getty Images; ABC/ Getty Images

All other photos courtesy ABC Photo Archives

QUIZ ANSWERS (pg. 96) 1.A, 2.C, 3.C, 4.B, 5.A, 6.B, 7.C, 8.A, 9.A, 10.B

PEOPLE
President Leah Wyar
Editor Wendy Naugle
VP/Group General Manager, Digital Zoe Ruderman
Creative Director Andrea Dunham
Director of Photography Ilana Schweber
Director of Editorial Operations Alexandra Brez

PEOPLE BOOKS
Editor Allison Adato
Edition Editors Carolyn Hinsey, Rich Sands
Art Director Greg Monfries
Photo Editor C. Tiffany Lee
Contributing Photo Editor Louis Pearlman
Contributing Writer Steve Dougherty
Deputy Art Director Lisa Kennedy
Reporters Gillian Aldrich, Stewart Allen, Mary Hart
Copy Desk Joanann Scali (Chief), James Bradley (Deputy), Gabrielle Danchick, Rich Donnelly, Shakthi Jothianandan, Matt Weingarden (Copy Editors)
Production Designer Lori Cervone
Premedia Trafficking Supervisor Sarah Schuster
Premedia Imaging Specialist Don Atkinson
Color Quality Analyst Sara Luckey

PEOPLE Public Relations Marnie Perez, Julie Farin

DOTDASH MEREDITH PREMIUM PUBLISHING
Vice President & General Manager Jeremy Biloon
Vice President, Group Editorial Director Stephen Orr
Senior Director, Brand Marketing Jean Kennedy
Associate Director, Brand Marketing Katherine Barnet

Editorial Director Kostya Kennedy
Creative Director Gary Stewart
Director of Photography Christina Lieberman
Editorial Operations Director Jamie Roth Major
Manager, Editorial Operations Gina Scauzillo
Associate Manager, Editorial Operations Ariel Davis
Special thanks Gabby Amello, Brad Beatson, Céline Wojtala

THE QUIZ

How Well Do You Know *GH*?

2 WHO KILLED LORENZO ALCAZAR?

- ❑ A. Luis Alcazar
- ❑ B. Skye Quartermaine
- ❑ C. Jason Morgan

1 WHY WAS SCOTTY ARRESTED FOR MURDER IN 1980?

- ❑ A. He punched Luke, who fell into the water off Frank Smith's yacht and was presumed dead
- ❑ B. He killed his stepmother, Meg, while she was having a drunken argument with his father, Lee
- ❑ C. Heather faked her death to frame him after he dumped her

3 WHAT WERE ROY DiLUCCA'S LAST WORDS TO HIS FIANCÉE, BOBBIE SPENCER, BEFORE HE 'DIED' IN A SHOOT-OUT IN 1979?

- ❑ A. "Protect Luke"
- ❑ B. "Leave the gun, take the cannoli"
- ❑ C."I love you"

4 HOW WAS DR. STEVE HARDY PARALYZED?

- ❑ A. In a car accident with Audrey
- ❑ B. He fell down the hospital stairs
- ❑ C. He caught Lassa fever at the hospital

5 WHERE DID FRISCO BUY THE AZTEC RING THAT INTRODUCED HIM TO FELICIA (WHO SNUCK INTO HIS ROOM TO STEAL IT)?

- ❑ A. An art fair
- ❑ B. Central Mexico
- ❑ C. Ye Ole Aztec Store

6 WHAT BROUGHT ALEXIS DAVIS TO PORT CHARLES IN 1996?

- ❑ A. She was dating Dr. Pierce Dorman
- ❑ B. She was hired to defend Kevin Collins for stalking Felicia
- ❑ C. Mapquest

7 WHERE DID DR. PORTIA ROBINSON WORK BEFORE COMING TO GH?

- ❑ A. The free clinic
- ❑ B. Harmony Maine
- ❑ C. Mercy Hospital

9 WHO HELPED EX-MADAME RUBY ANDERSON GET A JOB AT THE HOSPITAL?

- ❑ A. Nurse Jessie Brewer
- ❑ B. Nurse Bobbie Spencer
- ❑ C. An ex-hooker who worked for Ruby

10 WHAT DID ROBIN CALL ANNA BEFORE IT WAS REVEALED THAT ANNA WAS HER MOTHER?

- ❑ A. Dancer
- ❑ B. Luv
- ❑ C. Hey you

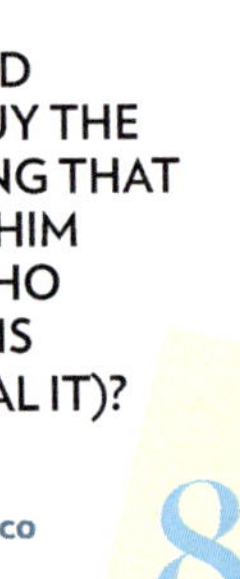

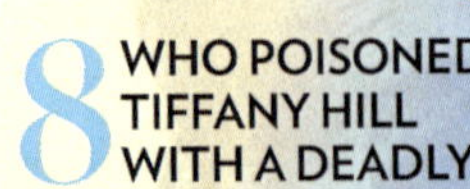

8 WHO POISONED TIFFANY HILL WITH A DEADLY VIRUS IN 1991?

- ❑ A. Cesar Faison
- ❑ B. Victor Cassadine
- ❑ C. Sean Donely's ex-wife